Political
Issues

CONTEMPORARY NATIVE AMERICAN ISSUES

Economic Issues and Development

Education and Language Restoration

Media Images and Representations

Political Issues

Sacred Sites and Repatriation

Social Life and Issues

Political Issues

Deborah Welch
Director of the Public History Program/
Associate Professor of History,
Longwood University

Foreword by
Walter Echo-Hawk
Senior Staff Attorney, Native American Rights Fund

Introduction by
Paul Rosier
Assistant Professor of History, Villanova University

CHELSEA HOUSE
PUBLISHERS

CHELSEA HOUSE PUBLISHERS

VP, NEW PRODUCT DEVELOPMENT   Sally Cheney
DIRECTOR OF PRODUCTION   Kim Shinners
CREATIVE MANAGER Takeshi Takahashi
MANUFACTURING MANAGER   Diann Grasse

Staff for POLITICAL ISSUES

EXECUTIVE EDITOR Lee Marcott
EDITOR Christian Green
PRODUCTION EDITOR Bonnie Cohen
PHOTO EDITOR Sarah Bloom
SERIES AND COVER DESIGNER Takeshi Takahashi
LAYOUT EJB Publishing Services

First Printing

9 8 7 6 5 4 3 2 1

Library of Congress Cataloging-in-Publication Data

Welch, Deborah, 1952-
  Political issues / Deborah Welch.
      p. cm. — (Contemporary Native American issues)
  Includes bibliographical references and index.
  ISBN 0-7910-7972-4 (hard cover)
  1. Indians of North America—Politics and government. 2. Indians of North
America—Government relations. 3. Indians of North America—Tribal citizen-
ship. 4. Federally recognized Indian tribes—North America. I. Title. II. Series.
  E98.T77W45 2005
  323.1197'073—dc22

                                   2005008831

Contents

Foreword

Walter Echo-Hawk

Native Americans share common aspirations, and a history and fate with indigenous people around the world. International law defines indigenous peoples as non-European populations who resided in lands colonized by Europeans before the colonists arrived. The United Nations estimates that approximately 300 million persons worldwide are variously known as tribal, Native, aboriginal, or indigenous. From 1492 to 1945, European nations competed to conquer, colonize, and Christianize the rest of the world. Indigenous peoples faced a difficult, life-altering experience, because colonization invariably meant the invasion of their homelands, appropriation of their lands, destruction of their habitats and ways of life, and sometimes genocide.

Though colonialism was repudiated and most colonies achieved independence, the circumstances of indigenous peoples has not improved in countries where newly independent nations adopted the preexisting colonial system for dealing with indigenous peoples. In such nations, colonial patterns still exist. The paramount challenge to human rights in these nations, including our own, is to find just ways to protect the human, political, cultural, and property rights of their indigenous people.

Contemporary issues, including those of culture, can be understood against the backdrop of colonialism and the closely related need to strengthen laws to protect indigenous rights. For example, colonists invariably retained close cultural ties to their distant homelands and rarely adopted their indigenous neighbors' values, cultures, or ways of looking at Mother Earth. Instead, they imposed their cultures, languages, and religions upon tribal people through the use of missionaries, schools, soldiers, and governments.

In the mid-1800s, U.S. government policymakers used the "Vanishing Red Man" theory, which was advanced by anthropologists at the time, as justification for the forcible removal of Native American tribes and for taking their lands. The policy did not work; America's indigenous peoples did not "vanish" as predicted. Native American tribes are still here despite suffering great difficulties since the arrival of Europeans, including an enormous loss of life and land brought on by disease, warfare, and genocide. Nonetheless, diverse groups survived, thrived, and continue to be an important part of American society.

Today, Native Americans depend on domestic law to protect their remaining cultural integrity but often that law is weak and ill-suited for the task, and sometimes does not exist at all. For example, U.S. federal law fails to protect indigenous holy places, even though other nations throughout the world take on the responsibility of protecting sacred sites within their borders. Congress is aware of this loophole in religious liberty but does not remedy it. Other laws promote assimilation, like the "English only" laws that infringe upon the right of Native Americans to retain their indigenous languages.

Another example concerns indigenous property rights. The *very* purpose of colonialism was to provide riches, property, and resources for European coffers. To that end, a massive one-way transfer of property from indigenous to nonindigenous hands occurred in most colonies. This included land, natural resources, and personal property (called *artifacts* by anthropologists). Even dead bodies (called *specimens* or *archaeological resources* by anthropologists) were dug up and carried away. The appropriation has been extended to intellectual property: aboriginal plant and animal knowledge patented by corporations; tribal names, art, and symbols converted into trademarks; and religious beliefs and practices *borrowed* by members of the New Age movement. Even tribal identities have been taken by "wannabes" masquerading as Native Americans for personal, professional, or commercial gain. In beleaguered Native eyes, little else is left to take. Native legal efforts attempt to stem and reverse this one-way transfer of property and protect what little remains.

Through it all, Native American tribes have played an important role in the American political system. The U.S. Constitution describes the political relationships among the federal government, states, Native American tribes, and foreign nations. Hundreds of tribal governments comprise our political system as "domestic dependent nations." They exercise power over Native American reservations, provide for their tribal citizens, engage in economic development, and sometimes come into conflict with states over intergovernmental disputes. Many tribes own and manage vast tracts of tribal land, extensive water rights, and other natural resources. The United States holds legal title to this property in trust. As trustee, the United States exercises significant power over the lives of Native Americans and their communities; and it is responsible for their well-being. These "nations within nations" are not found on international maps and are invisible to many in our own country.

Prior to 1900, about five hundred treaties between Native American tribes and the United States were duly ratified by the Senate and signed into law by the president. Treaties contain hard-fought agreements that were earned on American battlefields and made between Native American tribes and the United States. They opened vast expanses of Native American land to white settlement, protected remaining Native property, and created the political relationships with the U.S. government that remain to this day. As President George H.W. Bush said during his inaugural address in 1989, "great nations like great men must keep their word." Though many treaties were broken, many promises are honored by the United States today and upheld by federal courts.

The history, heritage, and aspirations of Native Americans create many challenges today. Concern for tribal sovereignty, self-determination, and cultural survival are familiar among Native Americans. Their struggles to protect treaty rights (such as hunting, fishing, and gathering rights), achieve freedom of religion, and protect Mother Earth (including land, resources, and habitat) are commonplace challenges, and sometimes include the task of repatriating dead relatives from museums. Each year, Congress passes laws affecting vital Native interests and the Supreme Court decides crucial cases. The hardships that Native Americans have endured to keep their identity are little known to many Americans. From the times of Red Cloud, Seattle, and Chief Joseph, Native leaders have fought to achieve these freedoms for their people. These ideals even today motivate many Native American soldiers to fight for our country in distant lands, like Iraq and Afghanistan, with the hope that the principles fought for abroad will be granted to their relatives at home.

Today, vibrant Native American communities make significant contributions to our rich national heritage. Evidence of this can be found in the recently opened National Museum of the American Indian, in Washington, D.C. It is also found throughout the pages of *Native Peoples* magazine and other Native media. It fills the best galleries, museums, and auction houses. It can be seen in the art, dance, music, philosophy, religion, literature, and film made by Native Americans, which rank among the world's finest. Visitors crowd tribal casinos and other enterprises that dot Native American reservations in growing numbers. Tribal governments, courts, and agencies are more sophisticated than ever before. Native American-controlled schools and colleges are restoring the importance of culture, traditions, and elders in education, and instill Native pride in students. The determination to retain indigenous cultures can be seen through the resurgence of tribal language, culture, and religious ceremonial life.

Yet many old problems persist. Too many Native Americans are impoverished and in poor health; living at the very bottom of almost all socioeconomic indicators and often in violence-ridden communities where disease, such as AIDS, knows no racial or cultural boundaries. Some socioeconomic problems stem from the aftermath of colonization of Native lands, peoples, and resources, or from efforts to stamp out Native culture and religion. Others stem from prejudice and hostility against Native people that has long characterized race relations in the United States.

As our nation matures, we must reject, once and for all, harmful policies and notions of assimilation and ethnocentrism, and embrace cultural relativism in our relations with the Native peoples who comprise our diverse society. History teaches where racial stereotypes, myths, and fictions prevail, human rights violations soon follow. But social change comes slowly and ethnocentrism remains deeply rooted in mass media and other corners of society. To little avail, Native people have told Hollywood to stop stereotyping Native Americans, protested against harmful racial stereotypes used by groups like the "Redskin" football team, and requested appropriate coverage of Native issues by the mainstream media. Native life is far different than how it has been depicted in the movies and by school and professional mascots.

Regrettably, schools do not teach us about Native Americans; textbooks largely ignore the subject. Sidebar information is provided only when Pilgrims or other American heroes are discussed, but Native Americans mostly "disappear" after dining with Pilgrims, leaving students to wonder about their fate. As a result, the people who met Columbus, Coronado, Custer, and Lewis and Clark are still here, but remain a mystery to legislators, policymakers, and judges who decide vital Native interests. Those interests are too often overlooked, marginalized, or subordinated by the rest of society. The widespread lack of education and information is the most serious problem confronting America's Native people today.

CONTEMPORARY NATIVE AMERICAN ISSUES will help remedy the information gap and enable youth to better understand the issues mentioned above. We are fortunate to have comprehensive data compiled in this series for students. Armed with facts, this generation can address Native American challenges justly.

Walter R. Echo-Hawk
Boulder, Colorado
March 2005

Introduction

Paul Rosier

During the mid-1970s, I attended Swarthmore High School in suburban Philadelphia, Pennsylvania. There, I learned little about Native Americans other than that they had lived in teepees, hunted buffalo, and faced great hardships in adapting to modern life at the end of the nineteenth century. But I learned nothing about Native Americans' experiences in the twentieth century. And as a member of the Tomahawks, the high school football team, I was constantly reminded that Native Americans had been violent and had used primitive weapons like tomahawks. Movies and television shows reinforced these notions in my young and impressionable mind.

It is my experience from teaching Native American history at the university level that students in middle and high schools across the country, have not, with some exceptions, learned much more about Native Americans in the twentieth century than I did thirty years ago. Several years ago, one of my students asked me if Native Americans still live in tepees. He and many others like him continue to be presented with a limited and biased interpretation of Native Americans, largely from popular culture, especially sports, where professional teams, such as the Washington Redskins, and mascots, such as the University of Illinois' Chief Illiniwek, continue to portray Native Americans as historical objects, not as citizens of this nation and as members of distinct tribal communities.

In 1990, President George H.W. Bush approved a joint resolution of Congress that designated November National Indian Heritage Month, and over the following years similar proclamations were made by presidents William J. Clinton and George W. Bush. On November 1, 1997, President Clinton stated: "As we enter the next millennium we have an exciting opportunity to open a new era of understanding, cooperation, and respect among all of America's people. We must work together to tear down the walls of separation and mistrust and build a strong foundation for the future." In November 2001, President Bush echoed Clinton by saying, "I call on all Americans to learn more about the history and heritage of the Native peoples of this great land. Such actions reaffirm our appreciation and respect for their traditions and way of life and can help to preserve an important part of our culture for generations yet to come."

We still have work to do to further "understanding, cooperation, and respect among all of America's people" and to "learn more about the history and heritage of the Native peoples of this great land." The information presented in CONTEMPORARY NATIVE AMERICAN ISSUES is designed to address the challenges set forth by presidents Clinton and Bush, and debunk the inaccurate perceptions of Native Americans that stretches back to our nation's founding and continues today. For example, schoolchildren's first intellectual exposure to Native Americans may well be through the Declaration of Independence, which describes Native Americans as "merciless Indian savages, whose known rule of warfare is an undistinguished destruction of all ages, sexes, and conditions."

The series' authors are scholars who have studied and written about the issues that affect today's Native Americans. Each scholar committed to write for this series because they share my belief that educating our youth about Native Americans should begin earlier in our schools and that the subject matter should be presented accurately.

Outside the classroom, young students' first visual exposure to Native Americans likely comes from sporting contests or in popular culture. First impressions matter. C. Richard King, Associate Professor of Comparative Ethnic Studies at Washington State University, discusses this important issue in his volume, *Media Images and Representations.* King looks at how these early impressions of Native Americans persist in film and television, journalism, sports mascots, indigenous media, and the internet. But he also looks at how Native Americans themselves have protested these images and tried to create new ones that more accurately reflect their history, heritage, and contemporary attitudes.

In *Education and Language Restoration*, Jon Allan Reyhner examines the history of how Native Americans have been educated in boarding schools or mission schools to become assimilated into mainstream American society. Reyhner, Professor of Education at Northern Arizona University, considers how Native Americans have recently created educational systems to give students the opportunity to learn about their culture and to revitalize dormant languages. Like non-Native American students, Native students should invest time and energy in learning about Native American culture and history.

This educational process is important to help Native Americans deal with a myriad of social problems that affects many communities in our country. In their volume *Social Life and Issues*, Roe W. Bubar and Irene S. Vernon, professors at the Center for Applied Studies in American Ethnicity at Colorado State University, review the various social issues that Native Americans face, including health problems like AIDS and alcoholism. They also consider how Native American communities try to resolve these social and health crises by using traditional healing ceremonies and religious practices that are hundreds of years old.

One very important issue that has helped Native American communities heal is repatriation. Joe Edward Watkins, Associate Professor of Anthropology at the University of New Mexico, examines this significant matter in his volume, *Sacred Sites and Repatriation.* Repatriation involves the process of the government returning to individual tribes the remains of ancestors stolen from graves in the nineteenth century, as well as pots and ceremonial objects also taken from graves or stolen from reservations. Native Americans have fought for the return of objects and remains but also to protect sacred sites from being developed. Such places have religious or spiritual meaning and their protection is important to ensure continued practice of traditional ceremonies that allow Native Americans to address the social and health problems that Vernon and Bubar describe.

In *Political Issues,* Deborah Welch, the Director of the Public History Program and Associate Professor of History at Longwood University, writes about how Native Americans reclaimed political power and used it to strengthen their communities through legislation that promoted both repatriation and the protection of sacred sites, as well as their ability to practice their religion and traditions, which the federal government had prohibited into the 1970s. Native American tribal communities have fought for their sovereignty for decades. Sovereignty means that tribal governments set the rules and regulations for living within reservation boundaries. Federally recognized tribal groups maintain their own courts to prosecute crimes—with the exception of major crimes, that is, rape, arson, and murder. Native Americans living on their own reservations generally do not need to obey state regulations pertaining to hunting and fishing and do not pay state income or excise taxes, though they are responsible for paying federal income taxes.

Tribal governments also help to create economic opportunities for their people, the subject of Deborah Welch's second volume, *Economic Issues and Development.* In this book, Welch examines the ways in which Native Americans have tried to create employment in businesses, which include ranching, mining, golf resorts, and casinos. She also considers how Native Americans have tried to develop projects within the context of their environmental traditions. As with other elements of their lives, Native Americans try to use their tribal histories and ceremonies to confront the economic challenges of modern life; to prosper by being *both* Native and American, while ensuring the health of Mother Earth.

Limited coverage of Native American life in schools, newspapers, and broadcast media has helped to perpetuate Americans' stereotypical views of Native Americans as either wealthy from gambling or suffering from poverty and alcoholism. The real picture is not so easy to paint and involves more than 560 separate Native American nations within the United States, which includes 4.1 million people who identify themselves as solely or in part Native American. The goal of this series is to explore the many different dimensions of the complex world of today's Native Americans, who are divided by geography, politics, traditions, goals, and even by what they want to be called, Native American or American Indian. Most Native Americans, however, prefer to be identified by their tribal name, for example, Lakota (Sioux), Blackfeet, or Diné (Navajo). And yet Native Americans are some of the most patriotic Americans, in part because their ancestors and relatives have died fighting in the name of freedom, a freedom that has allowed them to be both Native and American. As U.S. Army Sergeant Leonard Gouge of the Oklahoma Muscogee Creek community put it shortly after the September 11 attacks, "By supporting the American way of life, I am preserving the Indian way of life."

Paul Rosier
Villanova, Pennsylvania
March 2005

1

Early Political Development

Political issues involve two subjects: policy and politics. From the time of first European contact, the invading nations made policies to conquer, control, and/or maintain peace with the Indian peoples they encountered. After the American Revolution, the newly formed U.S. government began establishing policies that lie at the core of modern-day Indian law. The evolution of American Indian policy through Congressional Act, treaty, and court decisions is discussed in the first two chapters of this book in the context of Indian political evolution as Indian peoples sought to adapt to a rapidly changing world.

NATIONS WITHIN A NATION

Politics are, at heart, a contest over who gets to make the rules. Today, Indian peoples are engaged in politics on many levels. They are citizens of the United States, as well as of their own individual tribes, bands, or communities. The term *nation* is most often used to underscore the *sovereignty* of Indian peoples. When referring to one's tribe, it is common to refer simply to "the Nation." Indeed, the tribes continue to exist as "nations within a nation." This right to self-government has been guaranteed them by centuries of United States Indian law.

However, Indians find themselves with many identities. One may be Pawnee, for example, and also American—with allegiance and obligations to both nations. Indian people are also residents of the states in which they live and much of the political struggle over sovereignty today involves resisting attempted state inroads on the rights of tribal people to be self-governing.

The majority of modern Indian peoples do not live on a *reservation*. Rather they have made their homes elsewhere in the United States. They continue to be Indian, an ethnic and cultural identity that can be difficult to maintain while living as minority groups within American society. But the sovereignty of tribal governments is important to these people as well. Self-government ensures that the reservations will survive, providing a homeland for Indian peoples who live off the reservation to return to visit and take their children, often for *powwows* or other celebrations that reinforce their identity as Cheyenne, Choctaw, Apache, and so on.

Political issues for Indian people involve much more than interacting with federal and state agencies. Politics also exist on the tribal level as Indians engage in debate over who should rule at home. This has always been the case. Europeans did not introduce the concept of politics on this continent. For thousands of years before Christopher Columbus decided to sail westward across the Atlantic, Indians had been organizing the means by which they would govern themselves—a process that continues today. It is not always easy. Politics can be rancorous and factious. Finding the means to bring the community together and ensuring the welfare of all has always been at the heart of tribal politics. The ways in which Indian peoples accomplish this are as varied as the numerous cultures and societies that had developed prior to European contact.

Indian peoples lived in the area of the modern-day United States for thousands of years before the Europeans came. Their origins continue to be a matter of some dispute. The traditional stories of different Indian nations provide widely varying accounts of man's creation. The Navajo, or *Diné*, for example, tell of the first people emerging from several lower levels beneath the earth through a hollow log ultimately to arrive at their homeland, the land between the Four Sacred Mountains they call *Dinetah*. Other Indian nations possess their own stories to account for their presence on the American continents.

Significant evidence—blood types, language roots, teeth— exists, offering biological and linguistic proof that modern Indian peoples descended from hunting bands who migrated from Asia during the last Ice Age, more than thirty thousand years ago. As ocean levels lowered, the relatively shallow waters of the Bering Strait—separating Siberia and Alaska—receded, producing a land bridge. Over the centuries, as the Ice Age continued, grazing animals such as the mammoth and the bear, as well as their predators, such as the saber-toothed cats, began to cross. Following the herds and fleeing the ice, hunting bands of early people followed, unaware they were entering a new continent.

Permanent Communities Develop an Identity

Subsequent immigrations pushed the first travelers southward. By the time the Ice Age ended, these first Americans had already begun to develop economic, social, and political groupings best suited to the environments in which they found themselves. Early man traveled in bands, small groups organized along lines of kinship. For those bands settling in areas where ecological conditions of climate and soil provided relatively easy access to food sources, populations grew swiftly and more structured political rule evolved. Along the California coastline, for example, permanent communities began to appear, thriving on the rich resources of the ocean—fish and sea mammals—as well as the abundance of wild plants that could be gathered. Along the Columbia Plateau, Indian people soon learned to harvest the salmon runs, using dipnets, harpoons, and other trapping devices. The fish were smoked or dried, a safety hedge against hunger and soon a valuable trading commodity as well, bringing these Indian peoples along the Columbia River into contact with neighboring tribes.

Survival for Indian peoples in the Great Basin area proved more problematic. These people also relied on a staple diet of fish, supplemented by game they could hunt and plants they gathered, but scarcer resources in this area and on the Great Plains dictated that the hunting-gathering, and frequently nomadic, cultures would continue longer here than elsewhere. Evidence of their trade with their Pacific neighbors can be found in the seashells and obsidian mirrors (volcanic glass) found in the areas from southern Idaho eastward.

The development of plant cultivation, first begun in Mexico, spread northward after 5,000 B.C. In the American Southwest and east of the Mississippi, permanent societies began to evolve based on crops like corn, beans, and squash (what Iroquois peoples call "The Three Sisters"). Approximately three thousand years ago, ancient inhabitants of the area of present-day Arizona and New Mexico began establishing farming communities. The Hohokam (ancestors of modern-day Pimas and Papagos) people built elaborate irrigation canals for hundreds of miles, a strategy that enabled them to spread outward from the Gila River. The enormity of this task provides clear evidence that there existed a ruling structure to organize and oversee the work.

Near modern-day Phoenix, the Hohokam community of Snaketown was home to hundreds for more than 1,200 years.[1] Better known is Anasazi culture; their cliff dwellings in the

Cahokia, near present-day St. Louis, Missouri, was once home to between ten thousand and thirty thousand people—no North American city reached its size until Philadelphia in 1800. Shown here is Monk's Mound, which is the largest of several man-made structures that are now part of Cahokia Mounds State Historic Site.

Four Corners Area (where Colorado, Utah, Arizona, and New Mexico come together) are still visited by tourists every year. These architectural feats provide evidence of how large the Anasazi societies were. As many as fifteen thousand people inhabited the area of Chaco Canyon in New Mexico alone. Between 900 A.D. and sometime in the mid-fourteenth century, the Anasazis flourished, growing corn, weaving baskets of incredible intricacy, and creating pottery with detailed artistry. The latter provides evidence of a stability in Anasazi society that would not have been possible amid such a large population without sophisticated political governance.

East of the Mississippi, the transition from hunting-gathering cultures into farming communities, along with favorable

ecological conditions for crop cultivation, produced rapid population growth. As their numbers increased, older band structures gave way first to moieties, larger groups in which family
clans were ranked in order of prestige based on longevity and
tradition, and finally tribal organizations still based on kinship.
In the lower Mississippi Valley, more complex social organizations first appeared around 700 A.D. The mound builders
spread their influence throughout the Southeast and, like the
people of the Southwest, constructed enormous communities.
Cahokia, near modern-day St. Louis, boasted a population of
ten thousand to thirty thousand people, roughly the same size
as London at the same time period. Cahokia served as a major
trading center for the exchange of copper from the Great Lakes
(valued for fish-hooks and jewelry-making), obsidian mirrors,
and other goods, but it is the large mounds of the former city
that provide the principal evidence of its influence and the
powerful chief structures that had emerged.

In societies based on kinship, one's identity with an elite
family marked one's status within the group. Competition for
valuable resources also forced different Indian peoples to come
together in tribal structures based on common language and a
sense of identity. At the time of contact, more than three hundred different languages were spoken in the lands encompassing
the present-day United States. Such diversity would appear to be
an impediment to trade, especially among Indian peoples who
developed no written languages, relying instead upon oral mem-
ories handed down through generations of storytellers. But as
the tribes grew, so did their military might. More powerful tribes
imposed their languages on other groups. On the southern
plains, for example, Comanche hegemony was so well established that most of their neighboring tribes adopted the language, at least for use in negotiating trade and peace agreements.
Much like European diplomats conducted all business in French
during the nineteenth century, on the southern Great Plains, the
Comanche language served as the *lingua franca*.[2]

Other tools were developed for intertribal communication among leaders of Indian bands, tribes, and nations. Wampum belts, with their red and black beads signifying war and white signifying peace, are probably the best known. The calumet, an ornamental pipe with a flat stem that was highly decorated with eagle feathers, was widely used to promote trade and diplomacy. Its distinctive bowl was made from red catlinite, quarried in the Great Lakes and highly prized. The passing of the pipe for the smoking of tobacco became an accepted ritual prelude to discussions.

Not all discussions achieved peaceful resolution, however. As tribes grew in numbers and competition for spheres of influence grew, war broke out. Some nations like the Cherokee became so powerful that they dominated much of the present-day Carolinas, Georgia, and parts of Tennessee, as well as Virginia. They built fortified villages, a practice also adopted in the Northeast by the Haudenosaunee or Iroquois nations. To put a stop to intertribal conflict, the Haudenosaunee adopted the Laws of the Confederacy, using the Great Tree of Peace as its symbol in the late fifteenth century. The resulting league was made up of the Mohawk, Cayuga, Oneida, Onondaga, and Seneca nations and proved to be a powerful force. Individual village leaders maintained an autonomy in times of peace but again a political structure built on chiefs and a council assumed responsibility for matters affecting the good of the whole and extending Iroquois power over a wide area ranging from Virginia northward to Canada.

Other smaller groups adopted the confederacy structure as well. In the area of modern-day Virginia, thirty to thirty-five Algonquin tribes lived in the tidewater area stretching from the Atlantic to the fall line at present-day Richmond, loosely tied together under the mantle of the Powhatan Confederacy. By the time the English arrived to establish Jamestown in 1607, the Powhatan probably numbered around ten thousand people. Here, as among other Indian peoples, clan structure

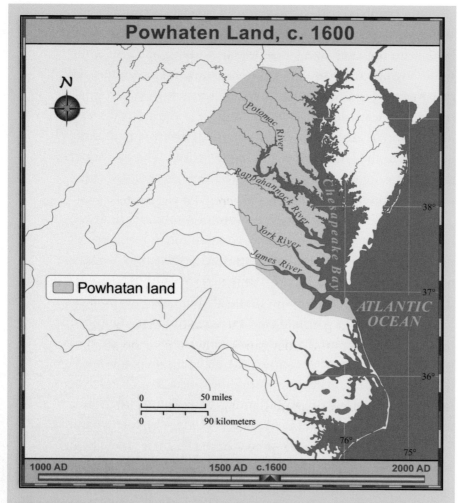

The Powhatan Confederacy, which was made up of at least thirty Indian tribes, including the Pamunkey, Mattapony, and Chickahominy, was centered around the tidewater area of Virginia and the eastern shore of the Chesapeake Bay, and had approximately two hundred settlements within its borders. The confederacy had a clan structure with a central chief (*weirowance*) who was responsible for leadership in matters of trade and war.

dominated, with a central chief, or *weirowance*, responsible for leadership in matters of trade or war. So powerful was Chief Powhatan's clan that when he died in 1622, his brother rose to become weirowance.[3]

European Perceptions and Policy

By the time of first European contact, America was not, as the Europeans insisted upon terming it, a *vacuum domicillium* (empty land); the description applied to justify the conquest that followed. Rather it was populated by millions of Indian peoples who over the course of thousands of years had developed viable economies and sophisticated political as well as social structures. Carrying the cultural baggage of their own political systems, the first Europeans attempted to foist terms on the Indian peoples they encountered. Powhatan, for example, was described as an "emperor" in early reports of Jamestown governors.[4]

Cortez's similar perception of the mighty Aztec leader Montezuma is more understandable. In any event, the Spanish were not interested in negotiating with Indian peoples. Conquest was their goal and the autonomous Pueblo communities they found in the American Southwest were too small to withstand the onslaught of Spanish technical superiority in weaponry.

The French faced a different problem when their early ships traveled down the St. Lawrence River beginning in the early seventeenth century, moving on through the Great Lakes region and into the Ohio River valley. Large confederacies and powerful Indian nations made armed conquest unfeasible. Moreover, the profit lay in trade, specifically beaver trade. Early on, the French recognized the importance of kinship to Indian political and social structures. Accordingly, they pursued a policy of intermarriage, sending small groups of trappers and later traders into what they viewed as the American wilderness. French policy permitted only men to immigrate with the clear intention that they would take Indian wives. Those inter-marriages produced new generations of Métis, children of mixed race who later served as valuable go-betweens negotiating agreements between French and Indian peoples. Many of the French men who took Indian wives never returned, preferring to

Pierre de Charlevois' Account of Indian Governing Customs

Many of the Europeans who first came into contact with Indian peoples following the onset of invasion failed to understand or did not have any interest in understanding that Indian societies already had well-established governments. In some cases, they insisted that Indians had no rules. In others, Europeans imposed their own cultural expectations on Indian peoples, identifying leaders as emperors, for example. As the centuries passed, these Europeans continued to be amazed at the degree of freedom under which most Indians lived. Even more startling to them was that Indian women also had a voice in determining tribal leadership. One example is an account written by a Jesuit priest who describes the egalitarianism and role of women in selecting chiefs that he witnessed among the Hurons in the mid-eighteenth century:

> In the northern parts, and wherever the Algonquin tongue prevails, the dignity of chief is elective; and the whole ceremony of election and installation consists in some feasts, accompanied with dances and song; the chief elect likewise never fails to make the panegyrick [sic] of his predecessor, and to invoke his genius. Amongst the Hurons, where this dignity is hereditary, the succession is continued through the women, so that at the death of a chief, it is not his own, but his sister's son who succeeds him; or, in default of which, his nearest relation in the female line. When the whole branch happens to be extinct, the noblest matron of the tribe or in the nation chuses [sic] the person she approves of most, and declares him chief. . . . These chiefs generally have no great marks of outward respect paid them, and if they are never disobeyed, it is because they know how to set bounds to their authority. It is true that they request or propose, rather than command; and never exceed the boundaries of that small share of authority with which they are invested. . . . Nay more, each family has a right to chuse [sic] a counselor of its own, and an assistant to the chief, who is to watch for their interest; and without whose consent the chief can undertake nothing.*

* Pierre de Charlevois, "Journal of a Voyage to North America" (London 1761) quoted in Steven Mintz, ed. *Native American Voices: A History and Anthology* (St. James, N.Y.: Brandywine Press, 1995), 58–59.

remain among their wives' people as *coeur de bois* (those who run in the woods).

The image of the *coeur de bois* frightened the English who disapproved of intermarriage between races as much as the Spanish and established their colonies with women and children as well as men. Yet they also came to recognize the power of kinship. Sir William Johnson married into a powerful Mohawk clan, acting as mentor to his wife's brother, Joseph Brant (Thayendanegea), who became one of the most influential leaders of his day, a vital ally in maintaining the Mohawk alliance with the British during the American Revolution.

The Effect of Warfare on the Indigenous Population

The ongoing European wars led to increased bloodshed in America as the European nations called upon their Indian allies and provided deadlier weaponry with which to kill. In some cases, they used longstanding enmity between Indian nations, such as already existed between the Iroquois and the Huron. On other occasions, they threatened to withhold the metal goods upon which they had made Indian people dependent unless their Indian allies agreed to fight. In still other instances, they took hostages, Indian wives and children, who would be returned in exchange for the men's military service.

The presence of war on this kind of scale forced Indian peoples to adopt new political strategies. Most Indian nations had already sided with the French, recognizing the greater danger the English posed. The French, after all, had established trading posts over much of America from Quebec to St. Louis and into the Rocky Mountains. Yet they numbered fewer than 1 million at the start of the French and Indian War in 1754. By contrast, the English colonists, confined to only a narrow strip between the Appalachian Mountains and the Atlantic Ocean had already grown to more than 2 million. And they were beginning to spill over the mountains, greedy for the rich farmlands that lay beyond.

The French surrendered in 1761 but their Indian allies fought on. An Ottawa leader, Pontiac, aided by a Delaware mystic, formed the first Pan-Indian movement in American history. He drew together a vast force, persuading the tribes to put aside the issues that had divided them in the past to face a common enemy. The Potawatomi, Seneca, Wyandot, Delaware, Shawnee, Miami, and Kickapoo were among the larger nations that joined the Ottawa in continuing to resist English colonial aggression. In the end, Pontiac's strategy paid off, forcing the British government to negotiate a truce, a central condition of which was the Proclamation of 1763—a line drawn down the Appalachian Mountains that the English colonists were forbidden to cross.

Pontiac's confederacy broke apart as soon as its goals were accomplished. The British, their treasury nearly empty after more than eighty years of constant conflict with the French, were determined to keep the peace with the Indian nations. To that end, they tried to centralize policy, primarily to regulate traders who might, left to their own devices, cheat Indian peoples, thus provoking renewed conflict. Equally important, they were determined to hold that boundary line. British reasons were most clearly laid out in the Atkin Report of 1755:

> The importance of Indians is now generally known and understood. A doubt remains, not, that the prosperity of our Colonies on the Continent, will stand or fall without interest and favor among them. While they are our friends, they are the cheapest and strongest barrier for the Protection of our Settlements; when Enemies they are capable by ravaging in their method of war, in spite of all we can do, render these Possessions almost useless.[5]

British determination to keep the peace lay at odds with colonial hunger for land. Only a little more than a decade after the French and Indian War ended, the American Revolution broke out. Again recognizing the greater danger facing them, most Indian peoples chose to fight for the British. There were a few exceptions. Some nations, notably the Seneca, were divided over which side they would take—and paid a heavy price for it when General George Washington sent American armies to burn their farms.

Other nations, like the Cherokee, tried to stay out of the fighting. But the older chiefs, who had already ceded some land in an effort to create a buffer between the English colonists and their people, came under sharp criticism from younger men who saw this war as an opportunity to regain those lands. When a delegation of Shawnees, Mohawks, and others arrived to try to persuade the Cherokees to join them in an alliance against the colonists, a large group led by Dragging Canoe accepted and began attacking American settlements. Ignoring their chiefs and council, these young men started a war leading to an even more awful retaliation than had been sent against the Senecas. American militia units from the Carolinas and Georgia began laying waste to Cherokee towns and crops. To stop the destruction, the chiefs reasserted their authority and sued for peace, ceding more than 5 million acres of land demanded by the American militia before they would with-draw. Yet Dragging Canoe and the men who followed him refused to agree to what they perceived as surrendering and instead continued to attack settlements. When the Americans retaliated, they acted as they had with the Senecas, making no distinction between those Cherokees who supported the war and those who did not. They cut a wide path of destruction and in 1780 burned the Cherokee capital at Chota.

Thus the American Revolution divided Indian nations politically and destroyed the economies of many people, plac-ing an additional burden of refugees on the nations as they took in those fleeing the smoldering ruins of their homes and fields. It was a heavy price to pay for a cause that was lost from the beginning. Englishmen at home had little stomach for what was viewed as a war against their fellow Englishmen in the colonies. Moreover, the English treasury could not support another war. When General Charles Cornwallis surrendered at Yorktown, the English decided to go home even though the main body of the British army still remained in New York. But rebellions are hard to defeat. And the British parliament realized that it could not restore the goodwill it sought with its American colonies by killing her sons. By far, the better plan seemed to be to retreat, wait for the American experiment to fall apart, and then return.

The French and Indian War as well as the Revolution set in stone the adversarial stance between Indian peoples and the Americans, who now had won the right to establish their own country. Yet the founding fathers who drew up the Constitution in 1787 implicitly recognized the sovereignty of Indian nations by placing treaty-making responsibilities in the hands of Congress alone (Article I, Section 8). That Americans already viewed Indians as sovereign people was also recognized in the treaty process long employed. One enters into treaty negotiations only with another country. In 1784, the United States signed a treaty at Fort Stanwix with the Iroquois, establishing peace between the Six Nations and America. Similarly, the Treaty of Hopewell in 1785 brought an end to the war between the United States and the Cherokee Nation. The Northwest Ordinance of 1787 provided additional congressional guarantees that the new U.S. government would recognize Indian sovereignty and their right to their land:

> The utmost good faith shall always be observed towards the Indians, their lands and property shall never be taken from them without their consent; and in their property rights and liberty, they never shall be invaded or disturbed, unless in just and lawful wars authorized by Congress; but laws founded in justice and humanity shall from time to time be made, for preventing wrongs being done to them and for preserving peace and friendship with them. . . . [6]

2

Domestic Dependent Nations

America's first president, George Washington, had little love for Indian peoples. An admirable man who set many worthy precedents for the office of the presidency, he used every diplomatic tool he could devise to keep peace with all European nations, providing the new and still weak United States time to develop. Still, at heart, he remained the old general and one who had seen many of his men die at the hands of Indian soldiers fighting for the other side. He longed for retaliation but was wise enough to listen to the counsel of his secretary of war, Henry Knox, and adopt what became known as the policy of Gradualism in dealing with the Indian nations.

U.S. INDIAN POLICY

Gradualism involved using treaties, bribes, promises of aid, and, when necessary, threats of military force to divest Indian peoples of their lands. Primarily, this policy was pursued against people in the

Old Northwest Territory (the area that is today called the Midwest). Knox also hoped to begin to acculturate Indian peoples to Anglo society. But the responsibility for Indian Affairs still lay with the secretary of war, a clear indication of the adversarial stance the new U.S. government took. In 1824, John C. Calhoun created the *Bureau of Indian Affairs* (BIA) in the war department, which was headed by a commissioner of Indian affairs who was responsible for developing and overseeing Indian policy. Not until 1849 would the BIA be transferred to the authority of the newly created Department of the Interior.

After he was elected president in 1800, Thomas Jefferson continued this policy of Gradualism, adding yet another tool in the arsenal of weaponry he was prepared to bring to bear by asking Congress to appropriate money to buy whiskey to be distributed to Indian peoples before negotiating. Jefferson also made the removal of all Indian peoples east of the Mississippi possible by his purchase of Louisiana Territory.

Acculturation

Originally intending only to secure the port of New Orleans, Jefferson's minister to Paris, Robert Livingston, and James Monroe found themselves presented with an ultimatum. The French emperor Napoleon was willing to sell New Orleans but only if the United States paid $15 million ($450 million today) for the entire Louisiana Territory. Although the price exceeded the maximum amount Congress had allocated to purchase New Orleans, Livingston and Monroe threw their political fortune to the wind and agreed, leaving it to Congress to spend the next year debating ratification of that agreement.

But it was a bargain and everyone knew it. Having purchased the land and ignoring boundary disputes posed by Spain, Jefferson wanted to know what he had bought. He chose two fellow Virginians, William Clark, younger brother of Revolutionary War hero George Rogers Clark, and Meriwether

During their trek up the upper Missouri River, Meriwether Lewis and William Clark were helped by a French trader, Toussaint Charbonneau, and his Shoshone wife, Sacajawea, who proved valuable in both guiding them through the rough terrain of present-day western Montana and serving as interpreters so that they could communicate with the Indians of the area.

Lewis to explore the country. Much has been written about the famous Lewis and Clark expedition: their trek up the Missouri River and their trip across the Rocky Mountains with their French guide and his Shoshone wife, Sacajawea, all the way to the Pacific Ocean. In doing so, they went beyond Louisiana Territory, providing clear evidence that the United States intended to expand to become a two-ocean country. For generations of Anglo-Americans hungry for land in the West, the return journey was perhaps even more important as the expedition stumbled across South Pass (an opening in the Rocky Mountains through which a wagon could cross) and followed the Platte River back to the Missouri River—more or less by reverse route, outlining the Overland Trail.

Lewis and Clark reported on the wonders of this new land —which now belonged to the United States—to a president who was anxious to hear their findings. At the same time, they told him that much of the prairie land they had crossed was, in their view, a wasteland. True, good farming land awaited on the other side, but to get there one had to cross what became known as the Great American Desert: land too dry, too barren, too cut off from navigable rivers to make farming possible—in other words, land no white man would ever want. This land would be the solution to America's "Indian problem."

Shortly after the Louisiana Purchase, much of the land encompassing present-day Kansas and Oklahoma was set aside as Indian Territory, effectively ignoring the claims of the Comanches and others who already lived there. Now Eastern Indian peoples would be sent there as well.

This steady encroachment of American settlers onto what had been Indian land produced a political crisis in many Indian nations. Many blamed so-called "government chiefs" who, either in a drunken stupor or bowing to threats, signed away lands that were not theirs to give. But the *Allotment* policy, first instituted by Secretary of War Knox, of promoting acculturation by dividing Indian holdings into individual property, had only worse results. One man on his own could be more easily intimidated into losing his property.

Some Indian peoples bowed to the pressures of acculturation, seeking to transform their nations into Anglo societies. The most famous case is that of the Cherokees whom Jefferson sought to protect even as he was divesting other Indian peoples of their lands. To the Cherokees Jefferson sent teachers, blacksmiths, and other tradesmen. Whenever possible, his policy called for these people who would train the Cherokees to be single and male, hoping to hasten the process of *assimilation* through intermarriage. What followed is known as the Cherokee Renaissance, a period lasting roughly the first quarter of the nineteenth century, during which the Cherokees adopted Anglo dress, farming methods, and some even developed plantations and owned black slaves like their Southern Anglo neighbors.

In the Northeast among the Iroquois, Handsome Lake, a Seneca religious man, also sought to help his people adapt traditional Iroquois culture to the changing world around them. Like the Delaware seer who had aided Pontiac, Handsome Lake preached what anthropologists term a *revitalization movement*; that is, they should hold on to the best in their culture and reject what was evil among the Anglos, most especially consumption of alcohol. At the same time, Handsome Lake persuaded many Iroquois to adjust to the Anglo social system of individual land holdings and possessions.[7]

Certainly Americans made sure alcohol was in plentiful supply among Indian peoples who were all too prone to fall prey to its effects, resulting in both social and political chaos. "Once-proud warriors quarreled among themselves or abused their kinsmen, although others retreated into drunken stupors."[8] Disease continued to decimate Indian populations, as smallpox, influenza, measles, and other illnesses killed many and left weakened survivors. Traditional clan rule among the Shawnee and other nations were helpless to stem the downward spiral of despair.

Resisting Acculturation: Tecumseh and Tenskwatawa

Indian political systems had always relied heavily upon spirituality and ceremony to hold clans together. As traditional political systems failed to work, many looked to religion, preparing the way for the rise of the Shawnee prophet Tenskwatawa. Like Handsome Lake, Tenskwatawa preached that Indian peoples should shun American evils, especially alcohol. He went further, devising a new religion that combined elements of Catholicism, which raised Tenskwatawa to holy status. His teachings spread like wildfire among the Delawares of Indiana and drew followers from among the Shawnee, Wyandot, Kickapoo, Potawatomi, Winnebago, and other tribes as well.

Many traveled to Prophetstown, the holy village Tenskwatawa founded at the mouth of the Tippecanoe River, near present-day Lafayette, Indiana.

His most important ally was his older brother, Tecumseh, who sought to secure arms and ammunition from the British in Canada. At the same time, Tecumseh put together a mighty army, threatening to put to death those chiefs who signed away any more Indian land to U.S. officials. Tecumseh effectively transformed what had begun as a religious movement into a new political Pan-Indian resistance movement. He traveled widely, seeking support among all Indian nations. His arguments were powerful and straightforward as demonstrated in his address to the Choctaws in 1811:

> Where today are the Pequot? Where are the Narragansett, the Mohican, the Pocanet, and other powerful tribes of our people? They have vanished before the avarice and oppression of the white man, as snow before the summer sun . . . Will we let ourselves be destroyed in our turn, without making an effort worthy of our race? Shall we, without a struggle, give up our homes, our lands, bequeathed to us by the Great Spirit? The graves of our dead and everything that is dear and sacred to us? . . . Sleep no longer, O Choctaws and Chickasaws, in false security and delusive hopes. . . . Will not the bones of our dead be plowed up, and their graves turned into plowed fields?[9]

While Tecumseh was in the South rallying support, General William Henry Harrison took advantage of his absence to mount an assault on Prophetstown. Ignoring Tecumseh's advice to wait, Tenskwatawa led six hundred warriors in an attack on Harrison's forces camped on the Tippecanoe River. Although the number of U.S. soldiers killed that day outnumbered Indian losses, Harrison still won the battle. Tenskwatawa had promised his followers invincibility. The dead and wounded among them proved that promise false and shattered Tenskwatawa's religion.

In the early 1800s, the Shawnee prophet Tenskwatawa, whose name means "Open Door," developed a religion that appealed to many Native people. The religion forbade followers from eating European foods or wearing their clothing and it preached that Anglos were evil.

The War of 1812, which followed, took the lives of many Shawnees, including Tecumseh. The back of the mighty Shawnee Confederacy had been broken, thus clearing the way for American settlement of the Old Northwest. During the 1820s, most of the Shawnees were rounded up and forced from their homes in Indiana to Indian Territory. The election of

Andrew Jackson in 1828 sealed the fate of those tribes living in the South as well.

Removal

In 1830, Congress passed the Indian Removal Act, appropriating $500,000 for the president to use in treaty negotiations with those Indians still living east of the Mississippi to persuade them to give up their lands in exchange for new territory in the West. The debates that followed split many Indian nations, as some leaders, seeing no other option, argued that they should accept U.S. government promises of land, money, and missionary aid. Others chose to resist.

The Creek Nation in southern Georgia and Alabama had already been forced to cede land in 1814, 1818, and 1821. In 1823, the Creek Council passed a law, adopting for the first time the death penalty to be imposed on anyone who gave up more land without council approval. William McIntosh, chief of the Lower Creeks, was one of those who felt that resistance against the U.S. Army would be futile and chose to take the deal American commissioners were offering. He did not want to leave his home. But far worse would be to see his kinsmen die as the Shawnees had died only a few years before. Therefore he signed the Treaty of Indian Springs, ceding territory in exchange for land in the West. He justified his actions on the grounds that at present Americans were willing to pay. If the Creeks did not sell, Americans would take the land anyway. ". . . and the little band of our people, poor and despised, will be left to wander without homes and be beaten like dogs. We will go to a new home . . . till the earth, grow cattle and depend on these for food and life . . . and we shall grow and again become a great nation."[10]

The Upper Creeks rejected the Treaty of Indian Springs and the Creek Council ordered McIntosh's death. Warriors who set fire to the McIntosh home and then shot him as he tried to flee the flames carried out the sentence.

The Cherokee Nation tried to resist removal through the courts. In two famous cases, *Worcester v. Georgia* and *Cherokee Nation v. Georgia*, which reached the Supreme Court, the Cherokees argued for their right to remain on their homelands. The latter case established the hallmark of modern Indian law when the Supreme Court found in favor of the Cherokees and underscored the sovereignty of all Indian peoples with Chief Justice John Marshall's ruling that they had the right to exist as "domestic dependent nations."[11]

Jackson ignored the Supreme Court's decision and the Cherokee Nation, like most of its neighbors, split up into two groups: a Treaty Party led by Major Ridge and Elias Boudinot that signed the Treaty of New Echota and left for Oklahoma, and one led by John Ross that remained in the Southeast, only to be force-marched to Indian Territory along the infamous Trail of Tears only a few yeaars later. A few escaped, hiding in the dense Great Smoky Mountains of North Carolina. Thus, the once-powerful Cherokee Nation was also shattered and permanently divided.

A similar fate awaited the Indians of the Great Plains. The story of their resistance is perhaps better known, at least the version made famous by countless American movies. Almost everyone has heard of Custer's Last Stand, perhaps the most famous battle of the Great Sioux War of 1875–1877. The Dakota and Cheyenne people attacked in the valley of the Little Bighorn that June day in 1876 did, indeed, achieve a victory over Custer's troops. But the old saying, "win the battle, lose the war" applies in this case. Alarmed that a modern army could be defeated by "primitive man," the American public howled for revenge. Retaliation was swift and merciless as Congress rushed to appropriate sufficient funding to send the U.S. Army back onto the Great Plains and force all Indians onto reservations.

Many of the tribes were sent to Indian Territory. Some Arapahos were allowed to remain in Wyoming but on a reservation they shared with the Shoshones, who were viewed as friendly Indians by the U.S. government. Other Arapahos were sent to Indian Territory—another Indian nation torn in two. The Sioux were divided and placed on separate reservations, extending from Minnesota throughout North and South Dakota. The Cheyennes were consigned to Indian Territory. In an episode made famous by Mari Sandoz's book *Cheyenne Autumn*, and subsequently in a John Ford movie of the same name, some of the Cheyennes tried to leave and begin the long walk back to their homeland. The U.S. Army followed, of course, trying to cut them off. But eventually American public opinion swung in favor of those desperate people and the Cheyennes were allowed to remain in Montana but only at the cost of sharing a reservation with their hated Crow enemies. Thus the Cheyenne Nation today is also divided into the Northern Cheyenne and the Southern Cheyenne.

There was no single path to resistance. Some Indian nations, like the Crow and Shoshone, chose to cooperate with the U.S. government because they saw that as the only way they could save their lands. Crow Chief Plenty Coups explained that they allied themselves with American force, "not because we loved the whiteman [sic] who was already crowding other tribes into our country, but because we plainly saw that this course was the only one which might save our beautiful country for us. When I think back my heart sings because we acted as we did. It was the only way open to us."[12]

Thus, some nations were allowed to remain within sharply constricted reservation limits on what had been their homelands. Others, like the Navajos—who were confined at Bosque Redondo, a rectangular reservation in what is now northwestern New Mexico and northeastern Arizona that comprises less than one fourth of what had previously been Navajo land—were allowed to return home. But at least it is home—some 3.5 million acres of what the U.S. government viewed as largely desert wasteland.[13]

Still others, like the Nez Percé and many Apache peoples—

both those who followed Geronimo and the Apache scouts who helped the U.S. Army find him—were tricked into surrender with the false promise of being allowed to retain at least a portion of their former homes. Instead they were imprisoned, in some cases at St. Augustine, Florida, in others at Fort Leavenworth, Kansas, before they were ultimately sent to Indian Territory.

In a twist of events unforeseen by American policy makers, confining Indian peoples to reservations served to strengthen their political structures. To be sure, some conflict between clans jockeying for superiority continued, particularly among the Dakota peoples of the northern Great Plains. But many people looked now to their chiefs for guidance and, crowded together in Indian Territory, many bands that had existed, more or less, autonomously, were now forced to come together as a nation if they were going to survive at all.

By the end of the nineteenth century, many philanthropic groups, such as the Friends of the Indian, had arisen in the East. Well-intentioned, if culturally blind, they saw rapid acculturation as the only way to save Indian peoples from being destroyed. The major obstacle to that transformation of Red into White, these reformers believed, was the continuing presence of tribal political structures.

Allotment

In 1887, Congress passed the *General Allotment Act* (also known as the Dawes Act) in a major push to achieve acculturation. In actuality, it was yet another land grab as Indian reservation holdings were divided into allotments that were distributed to the head of the household. The surplus was sold off to non-Indian peoples. Private ownership, reformers felt, would induce Indian peoples to learn the values of middle-class Anglo-American society. It also broke the community and the power of the chiefs. The 1898 *Curtis Act* terminated the tribal governments in Indian Territory.

Some Indian peoples took their allotments but continued to practice longstanding traditions of communal land ownership, living together as they had always done, herding their animals from high country in the summer to low country in the winter. In an effort to stop this circumvention of intended policy, the reservation commissioners began "checker boarding" allotments. That is, they assigned 160-acre quarter sections of land to one Indian family, declaring the quarter sections around it as surplus. As a result, Indian landholders found themselves surrounded by non-Indian neighbors, making the old communal lifestyle more difficult.

Allotment remained U.S. policy between 1887 and 1934, during which time some two-thirds of all reservation land was lost. It fell to another young reformer to put an end to the practice. John Collier, a social worker who had seen the injustice of poverty in the New York City slums, believed he had found a better way of life when he visited Taos Pueblo. In his view, Indian peoples had developed cultures of equal, indeed, superior, worth to that of Anglos:

> What, in our human world, is this power to live? It is the ancient, lost reverence and passion for human personality, joined with the ancient, lost reverence and passion for the earth and its web of life.
>
> This indivisible reverence and passion is what the American Indians almost universally had; and representative groups of them have it still.
>
> They had and have this power for living which our modern world has lost—as world-view and self-view; as tradition and institution, as practical philosophy dominating their societies and as an art supreme among all the arts.[14]

Appointed commissioner of Indian affairs under Franklin D. Roosevelt's administration, Collier pushed through Congress the *Indian Reorganization Act* (IRA) in 1934. Despite its many failings, the act did bring Allotment to an end and attempted to restore tribal self-government. Title I of the act granted Indian peoples the power to create their own governments with all the rights inherent to any municipal corporation. These included "the right to elect officials of government, to adopt ordinances for the reservation, to create courts for the enforcement of ordinances to regulate the use and distribution of property, to levy taxes . . ."[15] Title I also directed that Congress would appropriate $500,000 annually for Indian tribal governments and that those tribal councils would have approval for all budgetary matters concerning Indian peoples controlled by the Department of the Interior.

Collier was, in fact, trying to turn back the clock, to uphold the principles laid down by the Marshall Court in their findings that Indian peoples were "domestic dependent nations." The goal was not to sever federal government responsibility for the tribes. Collier, like the Marshall Court, recognized that their perpetual minority status required that protection. However, he hoped to provide a necessary buffer from the states. The IRA included additional provisions designed to promote Indian economic development, create reservation schools, and improve health care facilities—all noble purposes. Yet, the act failed in its implementation. The bill's provisions were not extended to Indians in Oklahoma, where most of the land had already been allotted. The bill did not take into account Indian peoples who lived off the reservation nor those who did not belong to recognized bands and tribes. Nor did Collier recognize that many Indian peoples might oppose his plan to impose tribal constitutions on them. The reasons varied but a significant core of opposition arose among many Indian peoples who recognized that the IRA offered no real self-determination. It was, in the end, yet another U.S. government policy imposed by Washington and the Bureau of Indian Affairs.

Indian Opposition

By the mid-1930s, many Indian peoples had become educated in and acquired the knowledge that allowed them to function in Anglo society—through published writings, public presentations to influential groups, and testimony before Congress—and to demand true self-governance. Although well-meaning, Collier maintained the delusion that had guided many of his predecessors—that he, and not Indian peoples themselves, knew what course to follow.

One of his most vocal opponents was Gertrude Bonnin, the Yankton Sioux writer and activist who, along with her husband, Raymond, urged Indian nations to reject the IRA.

In order to gain the benefits offered by the IRA—money for economic developments, schools, health care, and so on, each tribe had to vote to accept a new constitution, reorganizing its government. Collier sent agents throughout the country with copies of constitutions already drafted. One of his agents reported the opposition the Bonnins had successfully mounted at Yankton. "I have since been pretty well over the reservation and everywhere I find that Bonnin has beat us to it."[16] Nonetheless, Collier insisted that the Yankton vote proceed. It did, rejecting the IRA by a margin of two to one.

Collier encountered similar opposition on other reservations. In the end, more than one-third of the tribes voted not to accept the provisions of the IRA. Collier had declared the passage of the IRA to be "Indian Independence Day." But many Indian peoples saw no independence in yet another federal policy in which they had little voice. To be sure, many Indian activists held high hopes for Collier when he first emerged as a leader in Indian reform in the 1920s, but once in power, he turned a deaf ear to those who offered advice, particularly anyone, Indian or non-Indian, who opposed him.[17]

Cultural Pluralism and Termination

Despite his failings, Collier did succeed in bringing the hated

Ira Hayes, who died in 1955, was one of six men who raised the U.S. flag on Mount Suribachi after the United States successfully took the island of Iwo Jima from the Japanese during World War II. A Pima Indian, Hayes valiantly fought for the United States as a member of the Marines.

policy of Allotment to an end. Only 48 million acres remained of the 150 million acres designated for reservations at the onset of the U.S. government's Allotment policy under the

Dawes Act. Moreover, the reservation day schools he established meant that Indian parents no longer had to send their children away for boarding school education. In addition to the traditional education in reading, 'riting, and 'rithmetic taught to children throughout America in these years, Collier encouraged the hiring of Indian elders to teach at reservation schools, not only to expose the next generation to traditional crafts but also to instill in those children an appreciation of their unique cultural identity. Whatever his shortcomings, Collier swung the pendulum of American Indian policy away from assimilation and toward *cultural pluralism*.

Collier's determination to safeguard Indian rights to live separately under their own governments could not survive the onset of World War II. In the patriotic fervor of wartime, few Americans could understand or support a policy designed to encourage the promotion of cultures within the borders of the United States that did not want to be assimilated. Many Indian peoples chose to fight for the United States, joining the armed forces and serving with admirable distinction in many cases. The Navajo and Comanche code talkers who successfully thwarted the Japanese attempts to intercept messages they could understand is one example. Another example is that of Ira Hayes, a Pima Indian who, along with four fellow Marines and one Navy corpsman, raised the flag at Iwo Jima.[18] Thousands of others fought as well. The tombstones recording their names can be found in Veterans' cemeteries on almost every reservation. Many of the young men who returned found it difficult to fit in once again into the communities they had left. War had changed them and they posed a challenge to the traditional political structures of tribal life.

The federal government began to prepare an even greater challenge as the pendulum of policy swung again in the post-war years away from cultural pluralism and back to the old goal of acculturating Indian peoples. In 1946, Congress created the *Indian Claims Commission* to find a way to end all treaty obligations to Indian people and destroy reservation governments. The resulting policy, known as *Termination*, was instituted as the BIA prepared a list of those Indians who, in their judgment, were already sufficiently assimilated and no longer needed federal protection.

As was true of past acculturation policies, this one was also essentially a land grab. Indian tribes in much sought after areas, such as New York, California, Florida, and Texas, were identified for immediate termination in 1953. Other tribes slotted for immediate cessation of federal recognition lived in areas with rich natural resources, most notably the Menominees in Wisconsin, whose successful lumber operations and thick forests were coveted by a nation anxious to feed the booming post-war housing and construction industries. Sheer greed was in play here, not concern for Indian welfare. The fallacy of promoting Termination as yet another federal act of benevolence for its Indian people is most striking in the U.S. government's termination of the Seminoles in Florida. The BIA commissioners declared the Seminole people ready and able to live as middle-class Americans, although few of them spoke English and were so poor that most didn't even own a pair of shoes.

Termination removed all federal laws that protected Indian people from the greed of the states in which they lived. Wisconsin wanted Menominee timber. Florida wanted Seminole land to develop holiday resorts. Many Americans who had relocated to the Pacific Coast areas to work in the wartime aircraft industry wanted to stay. Land prices rose rapidly. As a result, California and Oregon Indian peoples found themselves slotted for Termination as well.

To deal with the vast numbers of Indians they had made homeless, Termination included a federal relocation program that utilized old buses to round up Indian families, taking them to the nearest city where they were promised help in locating jobs and housing. These promises were not kept. Instead, Indian ghettos grew in Chicago, Minneapolis/St. Paul,

Denver, Los Angeles, San Francisco, Phoenix, Albuquerque, and a host of other cities. Today, more than 50 percent of all Indian peoples do not live on a reservation.

President Nixon's *Special Message on Indian Affairs*, 1970

Throughout the 1960s, presidents John F. Kennedy and Lyndon B. Johnson called for new reforms in American Indian policy, arguing that greater attention should be paid to assisting Indian nations in developing the economic means to raise the standard of living on most reservations. President Johnson pressed Congress to create new programs for the benefit of Indian peoples and, indeed, urged a new approach to federal Indian policy, one based on "partnership, not paternalism." Termination had proven to be an abysmal failure. It remained for President Nixon to demand an end to that policy, calling upon Congress to reject forced Termination in 1970. But President Nixon went further. His eloquent speech endorsed the concept of cultural pluralism. Many Indians hoped that Nixon's words would usher in a new era of self-determination, one in which the right of Indian peoples to decide their own futures would be respected by the federal government. Nixon stated:

> . . . the story of the Indian in America is something more than the record of the white man's frequent aggression, broken agreements, intermittent remorse, and prolonged failure. It is a record also of endurance, of survival, of adaptation and creativity in the face of overwhelming obstacles. It is a record of enormous contributions to this country—to its art and culture, to its strength and spirit, to its sense of history and its sense of purpose.
>
> It is long past time that the Indian policies of the Federal government began to recognize and build upon the capacities and insights of the Indian people. Both as a matter of justice and as a matter of enlightened social policy, we must begin to act on the basis of what the Indians themselves have long been telling us. The time has come to break decisively with the past and to create the conditions for a new era in which the Indian future is determined by Indian acts and Indian decisions.*

* President Richard M. Nixon, *Special Message on Indian Affairs*, July 8, 1970.

The Civil Rights era of the 1960s and 1970s swung the pendulum yet again. In 1975, Congress passed the *Indian Self-Determination and Education Assistance Act*, which transferred administration of federal programs to tribal authorities. Self-determination seemed at last possible with this act. Greater autonomy in governing themselves had been restored to individual Indian nations and bands, those recognized by the federal government.

Since 1975, the U.S. government has followed a policy that recognizes cultural pluralism. But law and policy are one issue; politics is another. The Indian Self-Determination Act provided for home rule but did not address the question of who should rule at home. That was left for Indian peoples to decide. Different Indian nations chose varying strategies to develop both political and economic viability—to protect their land and resources from both state and corporate interests determined to profit from Indian acreage. But what of the nations left divided for more than a century? What of Indian peoples who no longer reside on the reservation? What was to be their role in tribal government? The various issues of Indian politics in the modern era and the ways in which Indian people have sought to meet those challenges will be discussed in the chapters that follow.

3

Pan-Indianism

The old dreams of Pontiac and Tecumseh to create a united front of Indian peoples that could withstand the incursions of first European and later Anglo-American invaders were resurrected in the twentieth century by Indian peoples seeking political reform.

In the late 1800s, many Americans who lived in the East began to form groups that sought to help the Indians, whom they felt certain were in danger of disappearing. These philanthropic organizations included the Indian Rights Association (1882), the Women's National Indian Association (1883), and the Friends of the Indian who, beginning in 1883, gathered semi-annually at Lake Mohonk in the Hudson Valley region of New York. Their conferences and publications pushed the cause of acculturation through allotment forward. Not all reformers agreed. Some, such as anthropologist James Mooney, opposed Allotment as shortsighted. A minority report of the House of Representatives' Committee on Indian Affairs protested:

However much we may differ with the humanitarians who are riding this hobby, we are certain that they will agree with us in the proposition that it does not make a farmer out of an Indian to give him a quarter section of land . . . the real aim of this bill is to get at the Indian lands and open them to settlement . . . If this were done in the name of greed, it would be bad enough; but to do it in the name of humanity and under the cloak of an ardent desire to promote the Indian's welfare by making him like ourselves, whether he will or not, is infinitely worse.[19]

The National Indian Defense Association, organized in 1885, argued that assimilation must take place but at a slower pace, in a manner to be determined by Indian peoples themselves. To these Anglo-American efforts to block the Dawes legislation, Indian peoples began to add their own voices. Lobbyists of the "Five Civilized Tribes" (the Cherokee, Chickasaw, Choctaw, Creek, and Seminole nations in Oklahoma) worked against the bill in Congress. Other nations passed tribal resolutions opposing Allotment.

Their efforts failed and the Dawes Act passed in 1887, which took political power from tribal chiefs and councils. But Allotment unexpectedly produced a new generation of political leaders. Central to the reformists' goal of Indian assimilation was the education of young people. To that end, Indian children were sent to boarding schools in the Midwest and Eastern states, often far from their parents. Indeed, separation was considered crucial if the children were to be taught how to act as whites. The largest of these schools were at Carlisle in Pennsylvania and Hampton in Virginia. By the turn of the twentieth century, new generations of Indian people, who were both highly educated and determined to be of service to their race, came to the forefront. The Indian rights groups established in the late nineteenth century, as well as the example of earlier Pan-Indian movements, helped create the models through which increasing Indian involvement in the direction of their own affairs might evolve.

THE BIRTH OF THE NATIVE VOICE

In 1911, at the invitation of Fayette McKenzie, a sociologist at Ohio State University, the first meeting of the American Indian Association—later renamed the Society of American Indians (SAI)—took place in Columbus, Ohio. Unlike other reform associations, which, although they did draw Indian members, remained predominantly Anglo, the SAI was to be governed entirely by Indian people. The Reverend Sherman Coolidge (Arapaho) served as the first president. Other distinguished members included Carlos Montezuma (Yavapai physician and activist), Charles Eastman (Sioux physician and noted writer), Henry Roe Cloud (Winnebago educator), Arthur C. Parker (Seneca anthropologist), Marie Bottineau Baldwin (Turtle Mountain Chippewa, one of the first women of color to earn a law degree in the United States), and others. These early leaders of the society hoped to organize the Indian voice for self-determination within the parameters of the Progressive Era, which stressed hard work, moral uprightness, and above all, assimilation into Anglo-American society. To varying degrees, the men and women who formed the SAI had internalized the lessons of their missionary teachers. They recognized the benefits of education and health care offered by Anglo society, and saw themselves as the bearers of these blessing to their race.

They had not forgotten the injustices suffered by Indian peoples, but the men and women who founded the SAI saw themselves as realists concerned not with the past, but with the present and the impact they could make on the lives of Indian peoples. This dismissal of the past is evident in the organization's description of its goals:

> . . . to bring together all progressive Indians and friends of Indian progress for the purpose of promoting the highest interests of the race and the individual. It asserts that any condition of living, habit of thought or racial characteristic

Carlos Montezuma, a Yavapai physician and activist, was a fervent opponent of the Bureau of Indian Affairs (BIA). He believed that the BIA's incompetence was the reason for wide-spread poverty among American Indians.

that unfits the Indian for modern environment is detrimental and conducive only of individual and racial incompetence. While the Society and its founders most sincerely appreciate the splendid elements and achievements of the old-time Indian culture, it realizes most keenly the inefficacy of using ancient ways to meet modern requirements.[20]

Dissension within the SAI

By 1912, when SAI's goals were written, the group's founders wanted to bring the benefits of Anglo technology, education, and health care to the reservations. The old order of tribal rule had, in their view, failed and Indian populations had dropped to their lowest point in the history of the continent.[21] New political systems had to be devised to take their place. What is clear in the forming of this organization by Indians for Indians was their commitment to the principle of self-determination.

Carlos Montezuma stood at the forefront of this fight in his cogent and constant criticism of the Bureau of Indian Affairs (BIA). He blamed bureau incompetence for continuing Indian poverty and demanded its immediate abolition. To that end, *Wassaja*, his monthly publication, adopted as its slogan: "Let My People Go."[22] Montezuma's criticism offended many SAI members, some of whom, like Marie Baldwin, were BIA employees.

Dissension among members regarding the BIA's role proved to be the first of many issues that would divide the SAI. Another was the question of peyote. Some members, like attorney Thomas Sloan, an Omaha Indian, defended peyote for its use in the Native American Church as an essential religious freedom. Others, particularly those coming from tribes where few belonged to the Native American Church, saw it as a new abomination that had no cultural roots in any Indian society. Leading those who opposed peyote use was Gertrude Bonnin, the Yankton Sioux activist who joined the SAI in 1914.

Divisions over these two issues weakened SAI's stated purpose to serve as the voice of Indian America to White America. Other problems arose to destroy this first effort at political Pan-Indian activity in the early twentieth century. As is clear in their statement of purpose, most SAI members felt that Indians should eschew the ways of the past. But not all agreed. The first issue of SAI's *Quarterly Journal* published an article by Laura

Cornelius Kellogg, a Wisconsin Oneida, in which she criticized Indian boarding schools' efforts to transform the Indian child "into a very average 'white man' just to have him 'white' in culture." Rather, she argued, Indian children should be educated in the heritage of both Anglo and Indian societies in order to create "a finer type of citizen."[23]

Other voices joined those of Sloan and Kellogg, who argued for accepting the best of Anglo-American society but not at the price of discarding what was good and unique among Indian peoples. Cultural pluralism increasingly began to take its place as one of SAI's principal goals.

The seeds of SAI's destruction were inherent in its composition. In fact, there has never existed a single voice of Indian America. Indian peoples were still too divided among themselves. Tribal identity held greater sway than a more general Indian identity. Gertrude Bonnin, who rose first to the position of SAI's secretary and later assumed the office of treasurer as well, certainly believed in the superiority of Sioux people. In her view, it was the Sioux who should speak for Indian America. One by one she orchestrated the ouster of SAI's members with whom she disagreed, but her most significant accomplishment was promoting Charles Eastman, a fellow Sioux, who was elected SAI president in 1918. That same year, she simply notified Arthur C. Parker that she was replacing him as editor of the SAI's *Quarterly Journal*, which was renamed *American Indian Magazine*. Bonnin thus carried out what was essentially a Sioux coup of the SAI.

Yet the question remained of whether SAI had any influence over American Indian policy. Carlos Montezuma, for one, believed SAI had become a useless, placating organ:

> The Society of American Indians has met and met. This coming together every year has been the mere routine of shaking hands, appointing committees, listening to papers, hearing discussions, passing a few resolutions, electing

officers, then reorganizing—that has been the extent of our outlook and usefulness for our race.[24]

The seventh annual conference of the SAI met in Minneapolis, Minnesota, in October 1919. Possibly hurt by his ouster the year before, Parker refused to attend. Thomas Sloan organized many members who supported his views on peyote to travel to Minneapolis where they overwhelmingly elected him as the new president. Thus the day that many SAI leaders, such as Parker, Bonnin, Montezuma, and others had feared— one in which the SAI would fall into the hands of the peyote-eaters—had finally arrived and created a permanent rift. The SAI continued on as a much-weakened group promoting cultural pluralism, but its original purpose to act as a national Pan-Indian organization had failed.

The National Council of American Indians

In the aftermath of the passage of the *Indian Citizenship Act* in 1924, Gertrude Bonnin set about to form a new Pan-Indian movement, the National Council of American Indians (NCAI). Its stated purpose was to develop an Indian political bloc by organizing the Indian vote, particularly at state and county levels to bring pressure to bear on politicians. Indian peoples, Bonnin argued, must seek more than merely influence in Indian affairs, such as had been the goal of the SAI. Rather, they must actively involve themselves in Anglo government to protect their rights to their lands, as well as their cultural inheritance.

Ensuring her right to lead, Bonnin became president of the new organization, while her husband, Raymond, took up the supportive role of secretary-treasurer. Both Bonnins immediately set about to legitimize the National Council of American Indians as the sole Pan-Indian movement, renting offices in the Bliss Building in Washington, D.C., the site of the Bureau of Indian Affairs and the American Indian Defense Association, and formerly the headquarters of the SAI.

John Collier lent his support and encouragement to the National Council of American Indians, announcing its formation and a call for membership in the California Indian Defense Association newsletter, *American Indian Life.*[25] G.E. Lindquist also announced the new organization in his handbook for Indian missionaries.[26]

Despite this initial support, the NCAI never attained any real standing as a national organization. Gertrude Bonnin penned some rallying cries for justice:

> A time there was when the protest of our race against injustice was voiced in the war cries that rose from the primeval forest. No less audibly shall this protest resound through the hills and valleys of our fatherland, echoing the farcarrying [sic] appeals of justice and reason, never to be silenced until the pledge of the Nation, made to us by the Great Grandfather, and sealed by our blood on their fields of France, is redeemed.[27]

Colorful prose indeed, but there was little follow-through on NCAI's promise to organize Indian voting blocs, although this stance did set an important precedent for future Pan-Indian activity. Traveling extensively throughout South Dakota and Oklahoma, the Bonnins were able to help defeat two U.S. senators whom they viewed as dangerous opponents of Indian welfare.[28] Thereafter, they seem to have confined themselves to local issues on the Yankton Sioux Reservation in southeastern South Dakota and, like many others, hoped that better days would follow with the appointment of John Collier as commissioner of Indian affairs. But the Bonnins' insistence on self-determination for Indian peoples soon forced them into conflict with Collier's implacable faith in his own vision for the Indian future. That self-confidence was unshakeable, leading Collier to write to Gertrude Bonnin at one point that he believed he was, at heart, more Indian than she was—a remarkable display of egotism for an Anglo man to write a Sioux woman. He went on to write "that

you do not own the Indians of the United States . . . judging by
the present course of action, if you did own the Indians, it would
be a sad situation for the Indians."[29]

Other Pan-Indian Movements

Additional Pan-Indian movements mobilized during the early
decades of the twentieth century. The best known is the Native
American Church, sometimes called the Peyote Church.
Today, its membership includes people from many different
tribes, although most adherents live in the West. The Native
American Church combines elements of Christianity with the
old vision quest, using peyote to achieve that goal. It promotes
sobriety, family unity, and responsible behavior—a reaction,
in many ways, to the sad state into which many Indian peoples
had fallen in the last decades of the nineteenth century.
However, the Native American Church has no political agenda;
nor did other Pan-Indian groups that were created in the early
twentieth century, which continued to exist following the
demise of the SAI and the Bonnins' National Council of
American Indians.

Many of these fraternal Pan-Indian groups arose in cities,
bringing together Indian people who had lost or moved away
from their reservation homes. The Tepee Order of America,
organized in New York around 1915 by Red Fox St. James and
Charles Eastman, first appeared as a type of Boy Scout venture
for Indian young people—there were orders for boys and girls.
Later, it expanded to include adults as well. Several orders were
established in New York, such as the Blackfoot Council (for
men) and the Daughters of Sacajawea (for women). Similarly
in Chicago the Grand Council Fire of the American Indians
was founded in 1923 "to revive faith of the Indian in the Great
Spirit and transmit it unalloyed to posterity; restore old cus-
toms, usages and traditions and keep them uncorrupted;
engender confidence among the tribes and encourage their cooperation . . ."[30]

In 1932, the Grand Council Fire was changed to Indian Council Fire and began distributing Indian Achievement Awards to recognize Indian leadership. Some of the earliest recipients—Charles Eastman (1933), Henry Roe Cloud (1935), and Arthur C. Parker (1936)—were well-known founders of the SAI. But while attention was paid to those political reformers, Pan-Indianism in the inter-war years and throughout most of World War II remained social and regional. Los Angeles, for example, boasted three Pan-Indian groups, all of which emphasized education but also encouraged their members to use the vote to protect Indian interests in an Anglo-dominated society. For the most part, fraternal Pan-Indian organizations encouraged a highly romanticized view of the Indian past with its leaders being given names like Sachem, Keeper of the Wampum, Guard of the Wigwam, and so forth.[31]

Political Pan-Indianism reemerged in 1944 with the formation of the *National Congress of American Indians* (NCAI). Throughout World War II, John Collier's policies of promoting cultural pluralism had come under increasing attack. It was clear to many tribal leaders that American Indian policy was about to swing once again—back to the days of enforced acculturation and destruction of reservation homeland. This time the U.S. government wanted to solve its "Indian problem" once and for all through Termination.

To meet this looming threat, prominent tribal leaders and other Indian men and women met in Denver, Colorado, to form the NCAI, with the goal once again to speak as the voice of Indian America. But the NCAI went further, working with the Indian Rights Association (IRA) to lobby before Congress to safeguard reservations, those rights guaranteed to Indian people by treaty, and the basic principle of self-determination—that Indian people had the right to live as they chose.

The Termination decades and the atmosphere of protest throughout the United States in the 1960s combined to produce new Pan-Indian groups, primarily made up of young people. The Civil Rights legislation of the 1960s and the formation of organizations such as the Office of Economic Opportunity brought new reforms to Indian policy, but the young were not willing to wait. Cherokee scholar/activist Robert K. Thomas described the mood: "As I look around at the Indian situation, it looks like one big seething cauldron about ready to explode."[32] In the early 1960s, a group of primarily college students broke off from the National Congress of American Indians to form their own organization, the National Indian Youth Council in Gallup, New Mexico. Its newspaper *ABC* (Americans Before Columbus) called for real

Proclamation to the Great White Father and to All His People

In November 1969, a group of young Indians, mostly college students and some activists from San Francisco and other urban areas, seized Alcatraz Island, the former site of a well-known federal prison that had been closed six years earlier. Their purpose was to call attention to the failure of the U.S. government to fulfill its treaty obligations to Indian nations. To that end, they issued a proclamation, carefully worded in the type of language that had been used in so many treaties to underscore the irony of those broken promises. Calling themselves "Indians of All Tribes," they established what they termed the *American Indian Center on Alcatraz*, calling it Indian land. The eighty-nine original members of the group were joined by others as time went on. Some visited and stayed for a short while to show their solidarity. Nineteen months after the siege began, federal marshals succeeded in forcing the fifteen people who remained to leave. But the takeover received a great deal of publicity in print and televised news accounts and served as a rallying cry to Indian peoples. The statement they issued (a portion of which is included) used irony to encourage other young Native Americans to believe that they should stand proudly as Indians, with cultures and societies equal to that of non-Indian America. Far from being second-class citizens, this proclamation reminds all that Indian peoples were the first Americans:

self-determination for Indian peoples; that is, that Indians themselves, not non-Indian bureaucrats in Washington, D.C., should be heard in the formation of policy.

Far more radical was the American Indian Movement formed in 1968. Indeed, throughout the 1960s and 1970s, many Indian peoples came together to stage protests—in 1970 atop Mount Rushmore, the 1972 automobile caravan to Washington, D.C., called the trail of Broken Treaties, and the 1973 occupation at Wounded Knee, South Dakota, site of the massacre of Sioux Indians in 1890. Perhaps the most famous of these events was the 1969 occupation of Alcatraz Island by

We, the native Americans, re-claim the land known as Alcatraz Island in the name of all American Indians by right of discovery.

We wish to be fair and honorable in our dealings with the Caucasian inhabitants of this land, and hereby offer the following treaty:

We will purchase said Alcatraz Island for twenty-four dollars in glass beads and red cloth, a precedent set by the white man's purchase of a similar island about 300 years ago. . . . We will give to the inhabitants of this island a portion of the land for their own to be held in trust by the American Indian Affairs and by the bureau of Caucasian Affairs to hold in perpetuity—for as long as the sun shall rise and the rivers go down to the sea. We will further guide the inhabitants in the proper way of living. We will offer them our religion, our education, our life ways, in order to help them achieve our level of civilization and thus raise them and all their white brothers up from their savage and unhappy state. We offer this treaty in good faith and wish to be fair and honorable in our dealings with all white men.

—American Indian Center, 1969

The American Indian Movement, which was founded by Dennis Banks and Clyde Bellecourt (Chippewa) in 1968, set out to reform federal Indian policies and address Native American grievances. During subsequent years, AIM staged a number of protests, including the occupation of Wounded Knee, South Dakota, in 1973. Pictured here at the end of the occupation, from left, are AIM leader Russell Means; Kent Frizzell, U.S. assistant attorney general; Chief Tom Bad Cobb; and AIM leaders Clyde Bellecourt, Pedro Bisonette, and Carter Camp.

a group calling themselves "Indians of All Tribes" who issued a "Proclamation to the Great White Father" (see sidebar on pages 44–45). The irony is clear in the title and in the document that employed the old treaty language to try and make a case for modern-day self-determination.

In light of the failure of Termination and increasing state demands for new policy, these combined Pan-Indian efforts helped set the stage for Congress to pass the Indian Self-Determination and Education Assistance Act in 1975, which transferred administration of federal programs to tribal authorities. Limited home rule had now become U.S. Indian policy. The political focus shifted away from Pan-Indian groups to the individual bands and nations. Today, the NCAI remains active as a Pan-Indian political voice seeking to influence policy-making—asserting its influence in state as well as national elections. At the annual meeting in 2003, almost all of the Democratic Party's contenders for the presidential nomination were either present or conducted a question and answer session via satellite television. The NCAI will continue to try and safeguard Indian rights on the national level. But the most difficult political questions facing Indians since 1975 are not being decided in Washington, D.C., but rather in the tribal councils of the individual nations.

4

Tribal Membership and Governance

In 1924, Congress passed the Indian Citizenship Act, a final step to extend the right to vote to all Indian peoples. The Fourteenth Amendment, added to the Constitution after the Civil War, bestowed citizenship on "all persons born or naturalized in the United States." But the amendment was written to apply to former black slaves. Fifteen years later, the Supreme Court made the distinction clear by ruling that an American Indian must separate himself from his tribe and undergo formal naturalization (much like an immigrant) in order to achieve citizenship.[33] The 1890 Indian Territory Naturalization Act made it possible for people in Indian Territory to apply to the federal courts for American citizenship while retaining their tribal citizenship. Recognizing the Indian veterans who had served in the U.S. armed forces during World War I, Congress passed an act giving them the right to vote in 1919. Five years later, citizenship was extended to all Indian peoples.

Though sovereignty is important to many American Indians, so too is their pride in being American citizens. Shown here is former Navajo Nation president Kelsey Begaye, who stands in front of both the Stars and Stripes and the flag of the Navajo Nation, which both fly on the Navajo Reservation.

SOVEREIGNTY AND U.S. CITIZENSHIP

Some tribes resisted the imposition of a citizenship they had not sought, viewing it as an infringement on their sovereignty. To that end, they refuse to exercise the right to vote that Congress gave them. They obey the laws imposed on all Americans. Like all workers, they pay federal income taxes. During the Vietnam War, their sons who were drafted into the military reported for duty, like the sons of other Americans. But their first allegiance is to their own tribe. The Onondaga Nation, for example, even issues its own passports with the Great Tree of Peace, that well-known symbol of the Iroquois Confederacy, on the cover.

Other Indian nations embrace their American citizenship.

At sporting events, schools, and in public buildings throughout Navajo country, one will find the Stars and Stripes flying alongside the flag of the Navajo Nation. Indeed, the sight of those two flags emphasizes the dual citizenship status of most Indian peoples—they are American, but they are also Cheyenne, Kiowa, Choctaw, or whatever nation or band into which they are born.

Native American Identity

The 2000 U.S. Census records 2,475,952 people identified as American Indian and Alaska Native living in the United States.[34] These numbers can be misleading, however, because the census records everyone who identifies themself as Indian. No effort is made to determine the veracity of the claim. The Bureau of Indian Affairs (BIA) restricts its services to those people who are members of tribes, bands, or communities that are recognized either by the federal government or the state in which they live. Those who can demonstrate Indian blood may apply for a CDIC card (often known as the white card), which, in turn, enables them to apply for tribal membership. Decisions about which individuals are eligible to become part of the tribe have been left to the individual nations to determine throughout much of U.S. history.

In 1846, the Supreme Court ruled that any person possessing "some" Indian blood and whom a nation or a tribe accepted as a member of their group might be considered Indian.[35] Forty years later, the Court declared that the Cherokee Nation could establish its own rules about who was and was not Cherokee, thus setting the judicial precedent that was applied to all Indian groups.[36]

The rules that Indian nations adopt to determine tribal membership vary widely. The term most often used is *enrollment*; that is, listed on the tribal rolls. Who is enrolled and who is not is the prerogative of each nation to decide. Some proof of ancestry (sometimes called blood quantum) is required, although, again, there is no uniform percentage adopted by all Indian peoples. Among the Eastern Band of Cherokee, for example, one-sixteenth blood quantum must be demonstrated. Other tribes do not deal in percentages but restrict enrollment to whether a child inherits his Indian blood from his mother or his father. The Seneca Nation restricts membership to those

Who Is Indian?

Everyone knows at least one person (and probably more than one) who claims to be "part-Indian," a statement usually followed by mention of a grandmother or some distant relative. The claim may be true. Centuries of inter-marriage have imbued many Americans with some modicum of Indian blood. But those genes do not make a person Indian. One must live in the community, adopt standards for one's own life, and be of service to the greater whole of one's people. Most importantly, it is the right of Indian peoples themselves to determine who is Indian and who is not. For others to attempt to speak for the Indian because they have some small portion of Indian blood running through their veins is laughable—even when that claim comes from the president of the United States, as Peter Nabokov points out:

> Constantly shifting for many people are notions of just "who is an Indian . . . " Sadly, the numbers game continued to govern the white man's notions of American Indian identity. After Indians noisily protested that President Clinton failed to appoint an Indian to his racial advisory board, the nation's leader made the point—hilarious to Indians who hear this particular boast all the time, as if it makes someone more authentically "American"—of announcing that he was one-sixteenth Cherokee. But the Oglala Lakota commentator Richard Williams reminded Clinton that "Belonging to a tribe, however, is about much more than a fraction of blood (a U.S. government-imposed standard). It is about keeping traditions alive and being responsible for our people. The needs are so great that members cannot be 'part-Indian.'"*

* Peter Nabokov, *Native American Testimony* (New York: Penguin Books, 1978), 446–447.

born of Seneca mothers. By contrast, the Arapahos enroll only those children born to Arapaho fathers.

This exclusion can often seem harsh, especially for a people for whom extended family is important. In a 1978 landmark case that reached the Supreme Court, a Santa Clara Pueblo woman, Julia Martinez, challenged the tribal council's ruling in place since 1939 that only children of Santa Clara men could be enrolled. Martinez had married a Navajo and based her case, in part, on earlier Santa Clara Pueblo matrilineal culture, hoping to secure membership for her children in the Pueblo. The Supreme Court upheld the Santa Clara Pueblos' (and by extension all tribal governments) "power to make their own substantive law in internal matters."[37]

Understandably, many people of mixed Indian descent felt their identity threatened by this legislation. Cases continue even today of people demanding their right to tribal membership. They seek recourse in the federal courts but so far the judicial precedent set in *Santa Clara v. Martinez* has been upheld.[38]

The sovereignty of the individual Indian nations is underscored in this power to establish their own citizenship. The greater majority of Indian groups accept children of mixed marriages (either with non-Indians or Indian peoples of different nations), provided one of their parents is enrolled.

Centuries of U.S. government policy designed to separate the Indian from his or her tribe has resulted in a large number of people who can lay claim to blood from different Indian groups. As one Cherokee grandmother writes:

> . . . my children are Cherokee, Kiowa & Comanche, and enrolled as Kiowa. Two of my grandchildren are Cherokee, Kiowa, Comanche & Sioux and Enrolled at Fort Peck. There are many children & young adults that may be 4/4ths yet of too many tribes to be enrolled in any of them.[39]

There are approximately three hundred American Indian tribes that the Bureau of Indian Affairs does not recognize, including the Abenaki, whose traditional home is northern New England. The Abenakis have established a tribal museum to both commemorate and raise awareness of their people in an effort to gain federal and state recognition. Shown here is Fred Wiseman, director of the Abenaki Tribal Museum in Swanton, Vermont.

Recognition of Indian Tribes

At present there exist more than 560 federally recognized Indian nations. The BIA does not recognize approximately 300 other Indian tribes. Some, like the Lumbee in North Carolina and most recently the Waccamaw and Pee Dee Nation of Upper South Carolina, are recognized by their states but they do not meet BIA criteria for federal status.[40] In the case of the Lumbees, they lack a common cultural heritage (language) and they never signed a treaty with the United States. Both are grounds for BIA denial.

Membership in a federally recognized tribe brings some

benefits—access to the Indian Health Service, preferential hiring in staffing federal program positions on the reservation, and eligibility for student loans. However, anyone possessing a CDIB (Certificate of Degree of Indian Blood) card demonstrating their Indian ancestry is eligible for health and educational benefits, whether a tribal member or not. Using those services becomes problematic depending upon where one lives. If one is close enough to an Indian Health Service facility designed for one's people, one may use it. This is not the case for the vast majority of Indian peoples who do not live on or near a reservation today.

In other instances, the federal government does not recognize a person's tribal identity even though their community does. For example, among the western Cherokees, blood quantum is determined by the presence of an ancestor's name on the Dawes Rolls. Many Cherokees resisted the Dawes Act and refused to sign up for an allotment or they were living elsewhere when the allotment process was ongoing and did not return to Indian Territory to register. Whatever the case, the descendants of these people cannot be enrolled today nor are they acknowledged as Cherokee by the federal government regardless of how much Cherokee blood they may demonstrate.

The numerous questions of who is and who is not eligible for tribal membership continue to cause dissension throughout Indian Country. The problem of identity runs even deeper for those who live apart from the reservation and has resulted in the rise of a number of Pan-Indian groups in America's cities. Here, various cultural traditions are merged into "a general sense of Indianness," enabling people to come together in Indian centers, churches, bowling leagues, softball teams, and other gatherings.[41] The most public of these gatherings both on and off the reservation is, of course, the powwow. These large festivities are held annually on reservations but also in major urban centers such as Chicago, Albuquerque, Denver, and Oklahoma City.[42]

Powwows always include dance competitions and exhibitions, along with booths that have Indian craft items for purchase. More importantly, they provide an opportunity for reservation and non-reservation Indians to interact with one another.

One of the most important benefits to tribal enrollment is the right it conveys to vote in tribal elections. Among some Indian nations, that right is extended to all whether they live on the reservation or not. Others confine the vote and other tribal services only to those who live in the community.

Political Organization

Government organization varies widely, a reflection of the different cultures of Indian peoples. Some, like the Cherokee Nation in Oklahoma, retain the office of chief, to be aided by a deputy chief and tribal council. In December 1990, the tribal council established a district court and expanded the tribe's police force into the Cherokee Nation Marshal Service. Like all Indian nations, these police must work with local law enforcement officers within their states. The Cherokees have a cross-deputation agreement with the fourteen counties of northeastern Oklahoma, which includes Cherokee land.[43]

The Seneca Nation of Indians adopted its title in 1848 when they abandoned the chief system and established a constitution that called for elected officials and three branches of government—an executive, legislative, and judicial. The Seneca people live on three areas of land in western New York, with the majority divided between the Cattaraugus Reservation along Lake Erie, between Dunkirk and Buffalo, and the Allegany Reservation, which includes the town of Salamanca. The executive branch of their government consists of a president, treasurer, and clerk who are elected for two-year terms and may not succeed themselves. The elected officials alternate between the two reservations; that is, a candidate living on Cattaraugus may be elected for one term to be followed by a candidate from Allegany. Tribal council is composed of

sixteen members, eight from Cattaraugus and eight from
Allegany. Their judiciary is organized into peacemaker, appel-
late, and surrogate courts.[44]

Both the Cherokees and the Senecas provide examples of
how traditional tribal government has evolved to meet modern
needs and yet retain their cultural distinctiveness. Clearly, the
Senecas based their 1848 Constitution on the U.S. model, yet
among their elected officials they included the peacemakers.
These peacemakers are legal officers, but their role differs
markedly from local judges in neighboring non-Indian communities. They exist to promote resolution, bringing all parties
together to achieve a continuing peace.

Similarly, the Navajo Nation relies on peacemakers but not
in any official capacity as members of tribal government.
Rather, they are available to assist in the resolution of disputes
to promote harmony. In all cases, the peacemakers are usually
very effective. They live in the community; they know the people involved; and thus are able to bring all parties to the table
to discuss the issues—sometimes for days, if necessary, until
they achieve a satisfactory settlement. Unlike non-Indian
courts, the goal of the peacemakers is not to assign blame or
punishment, but to effect reconciliation, maintaining goodwill
among the people.[45]

The peacemakers are not always successful, of course.
Reservation residents then have the right to take their case to
tribal courts. If not satisfied by the ruling they receive there,
they have the right to go on to the tribal court of appeals and
from there to federal district courts, the U.S. Court of Appeals,
and, in some cases, all the way to the U.S. Supreme Court.[46]

Responsibility for all governance and law enforcement is a
tangled web of shared responsibility among the tribes, states,
and federal government. The dual citizenship of Indian peoples means that they have access to the same rights and pro-
tections of all Americans, as well as the same responsibilities to
the larger nation of which they are a part. Indian peoples pay

federal income taxes. Their young men must register for Selective Service at age eighteen. But those who live on reservations or in tribal communities also come under the authority of their own governing systems.

In 1974, the National American Indian Court Judges Association listed four principal categories into which tribal governments fall:

1) **Representative**: These are governments elected by tribal members, using procedures outlined in a constitution that the tribe approved. The Ute and Jicarilla Apache people provide two examples of this kind of government.

2) **Representative/Traditional Combination**: Again, most of the tribal officials are elected but traditional leaders (designated by their lineage) fill some positions. These nations, such as the Red Lake Band of Chippewa, have a written constitution.

3) **General Council**: In this case, the members of the tribe vote on by-laws under which they elect tribal officers but those officials have no real authority. When issues arise affecting the whole tribe, a general council meeting is called and the tribe as a whole votes. The Crow Nation of Montana provides a case study of this kind of government.

4) **Theocracy**: This very traditional tribal government is practiced primarily among the Pueblo people of the American Southwest. The religious leadership selects the civil officials who see to the day-to-day matters of community governance.[47]

Other Indian peoples have formed governments that do not fall into any of these categories. For example, the Catawba Indian people of South Carolina are a federally recognized group but were terminated in the 1960s. Unlike some Indian peoples, such as the Menominees in Wisconsin, who fought successfully both for a return of their lands and their tribal governance, the Catawbas decided to incorporate themselves as a town. Their federally recognized status enables them to apply for grants made possible by a plethora of legislation passed in the 1970s and their township provides them with the authority to rule themselves on the local level.

Laws to Restore Sovereignty

The decade following the passage of the Civil Rights Act in 1964 produced a number of laws that were intended to restore some measure of sovereignty to Indian peoples, at least the ability to engage in a restricted home rule over their own affairs.

The 1972 Indian Education Act provided funding for public school education for Indian children. The 1975 Indian Self-Determination and Education Assistance Act went a great deal further, transferring administration of federal programs to tribal authorities. Tribal governments must still contract with the BIA for Indian Health Services, schools, and other necessary community services, but they operate those facilities, replacing the bureaucrats of the departments of Interior and Health and Human Services. In other words, Indian parents now sit on their children's school boards.

The 1974 *Indian Financing Act* made available grants and loans to Indian nations to encourage economic development. In 1978, Congress passed the Indian Religious Freedom Act and the Indian Civil Rights Act. The First Amendment of the Constitution guarantees religious freedom to all citizens. Nonetheless, many states continued to prosecute Indian people for some religious practices, which led Congress to make clear the federal government's intention "to protect and preserve for American Indians their inherent right of freedom to believe, express, and exercise" their religions, "including but not limited to access to sites, use and possession of sacred objects, and the freedom to worship through ceremonials and traditional rights."[48]

Of primary importance to many Indian peoples is the 1978 *Indian Child Welfare Act,* which restored responsibility for the social welfare of Indian children to tribal governments. Prior to this, federal, state, and county welfare officials could and often did intercede. Refusing to recognize the concept of extended family, for example, these bureaucrats would interfere when a child lost its parents either through death, health issues, or other circumstances. Invariably, the child was then placed in foster services with non-Indian families. Adoption proceedings always resulted in the relocation of the child with new non-Indian parents. The ability to protect their own children is perhaps the most important right tribal governments now possess.

The passage of these laws, most especially the Indian Self-Determination Act, was touted in Washington, D.C., as a new era of Indian freedom. Yet many restrictions remain and authority is shared between the tribes and the federal, state, and county governments. In some cases, tribal and local law enforcement officials have found ways of working together to promote the peace between Indian and non-Indian. The cross-deputation agreements are one example. A Hopi tribal officer could also be empowered with the authority of a county deputy. Similar agreements are in place for the Navajo, the Cherokee, and some other Indian nations. But again, their authority is limited to dealing with traffic offenses, disturbing the peace, petty thefts, and the many other crimes with which all law officials must deal. Major felonies (murder, for example) fall under the jurisdiction of federal officers, specifically the Federal Bureau of Investigation (FBI), who work in conjunction with tribal police.

The problems of shared authority between tribal governments and the federal authorities, as well as the state, will be discussed in chapters 6 and 7, respectively. There remains the larger issue of how tribal governments operate in the post-1975 era. Some scholars insist the Indian Self-Determination Act was no more than another version of John Collier's 1934 Indian

Rights Act. Perhaps so, but the law at least recognizes limited
sovereignty for Indian groups and restored authority to tribal
governments. But freedom always includes dissent. The Indian
Self-Determination Act restored "home rule." In the last three
decades, Indian peoples have struggled with the issue of "who
should rule at home."[49]

5

Tribal Factionalism

In the introduction to her book *Tribal Sovereignty and the Historical Imagination*, Loretta Fowler poses the question: "Why do the avowal of tribal unity and the demonstration of widespread political cooperation exist in the ritual sphere (particularly in the organization of powwows and dances), yet, in the context of tribal government, these same ritual participants commit themselves to contest political acts and undermine each other's efforts?"[50] In other words, Indian people come together for acts of ceremony or religion, but when it comes to politics, dissension is sharp and widespread. Almost no reservation has escaped the trouble that comes with a disputed election in the decades since the passage of the Indian Self-Determination Act. As stated in the previous chapter, reservation denizens have the right of appeal from tribal to federal courts. The U.S. Department of the Interior has been flooded with petitions to overturn elections, investigate and/or remove tribal leaders, intercede with decisions made by tribal councils, and take sides with one group against another.

POLITICS: A DIVISIVE ISSUE

That politics is a divisive issue should surprise no one and certainly the kind of arguments that surround every election are familiar to anyone who has turned on the television news or picked up a newspaper in recent years. Mudslinging, vicious charges, and counter charges make front-page news in every presidential, congressional, state, and even county election throughout the United States.

Yes, politics always produces rancor. But in the end, the United States is a republic with a written constitution and we abide by the election results, even when there is fervent opposition to the policies of elected officials. Why should American Indian peoples be any different? Of course there are going to be political disagreements. But the concept of shared authority between tribal governments and federal bureaucracy provides an avenue to keep dissension alive in Indian Country, as appeals wind their way through the courts. The result is often a stalemate with tribal officials unable to focus their full attention on the duties for which they were elected or appointed.

Social Issues Create Flashpoints

These intratribal arguments impede the unity necessary for Indian people to address the very real social problems that still plague them. For example, the National American Indian Housing Council's 2004 survey of Indian housing revealed that "83 percent reported 'substandard' housing on their reservation, although 59 percent said housing was overcrowded." The report goes on to state that the housing problems led to other societal ills, ranging from alcoholism to sleep deprivation.[51]

This report was released to coincide with the opening of the National Museum of the American Indian in Washington, D.C., in 2004, and called upon the federal government to do more to

Under the leadership of Chief Phillip Martin, the Mississippi Band of Choctaw Indians have been extremely successful in their business endeavors. Martin has reduced unemployment among his people from a rate of 80 percent when he became chief in 1969 to less than 4 percent in 2004. In addition, he has helped create thousands of jobs for his people and the tribe holds more than $1 billion worth of assets.

help ease reservation poverty. But the 1960s and 1970s legislation designed to promote greater Indian self-determination, both politically and economically, came to an end in the 1980s when almost all domestic programs were cut sharply. In any event, Indian peoples learned long ago that their survival depends on themselves.

Most tribal communities are working hard to develop reservation businesses to provide much-needed revenue. One of the most phenomenal cases of success can be found among the Choctaw Band of Mississippi, who are united behind the leadership of Phillip Martin, who was elected head of the tribal council in 1979.[52] In the 1960s, the Mississippi Choctaws lived in deep rural poverty: Ninety percent of all housing lacked indoor plumbing; one-third had no electricity.[53] Martin and the tribal council succeeded in drawing business ventures to the area, ranging from General Electric to Pepsico, Inc. Using funds gained from these enterprises, the Choctaws began their own businesses and invested the proceeds into building homes and roads, as well as ensuring scholarships for their young people.

Other success stories exist, many of which surround the revenues brought to tribes by casino gambling establishments opened on reservation land. But this issue has also produced some of the sharpest dissension. Some tribal members may favor gambling as a proven source of economic success. Others, usually those more traditional members who fear the inroads on Indian culture and society, oppose the decision. The temptation is obvious. Foxwoods, the Mashantucket Pequot casino in Ledyard, Connecticut, claims today to be the largest casino in the world—the profits for the Pequots are enormous. But for whom? In some cases, casino gambling has raised employment opportunities to the point where everyone on the reservation may have a job. Those Indian tribal members who oppose gambling and will not venture near the casinos often have to continue to eke out an existence as best they can. This dividing of reservation communities into *haves* and *have-nots* only underscores the political tensions.

Part of the background for these continuing divisions within Indian communities derives from two sources: 1) a long cultural tradition of political leadership that permitted freedom to individuals to follow tribal officials, or not, as they saw fit; and 2) the necessary period of adjustment to tribal governments with written constitutions that are comparatively new. Many of those constitutions were created after 1934 under the auspices of the Indian Reorganization Act. Others are still more recent and subject to frequent revision.

Among many Indian peoples prior to the twentieth

century, political leadership conveyed little real authority. Some tribes had peace chiefs and war chiefs. The latter were chosen in times of war, their leadership assumed for the period of crisis and then discarded when the battle was over. Peace chiefs were primarily responsible for the well-being of the whole. It was left to warrior societies, those clans whose hegemony was determined by longstanding tradition, to enforce compliance for the good of the whole. For example, on the Great Plains, these warrior societies brought the bands together for the annual buffalo hunt, when large numbers of manpower were needed, and led the fighting when war was necessary.

Dragging Canoe and the Cherokees

But dissenters have always existed. The case of Dragging Canoe, sometimes treated as a hero among the Cherokees, provides one example.[54] By the time of the American Revolution, the Cherokees had already lost much of the land they considered part of their sphere of influence to the steady encroachment of English colonists. In March 1775, a group of North Carolina land speculators persuaded the Cherokee chiefs Attakullakulla, Oconostota, and Savunkah to sell 27,000 square miles of territory, perhaps in a futile effort to buy peace. But many younger men disagreed. Led by Attakullakulla's son, Dragging Canoe (Chincanacina), these young warriors seized the opportunity offered by the American Revolution to challenge the authority of the older chiefs. They joined the Shawnees, Delawares, Mohawks, and others organized to fight for the British and began attacking American settlements. The chiefs had no power to stop them.

American retaliation, when it came, was merciless: they burned the homes and cornfields of every Cherokee family they found. To buy the peace, the chiefs were forced to cede another 5 million acres in Georgia, North Carolina, Virginia, and South Carolina. Dragging Canoe and those who followed him refused to acknowledge the treaties and split with their nation, building new towns along the Chickamauga River, calling themselves the Chickamauga Cherokees. This splinter faction continued to fight, which brought even more trouble to the Cherokees. In 1780, American forces burned the capital at Chota. By the end of the war, more than half of all Cherokee towns had been destroyed, three-quarters of their territory had been lost, and their numbers decimated by 10,000.[55] To stop the slaughter, the Cherokee chiefs signed the Treaty of Hopewell in 1785, their first treaty with the new U.S. government.

The case of Dragging Canoe provides an eighteenth-century example of the cost to the people as a whole produced by tribal disunity. A more modern-day example can be found among the Navajos with the story of Peter MacDonald.

Peter MacDonald and the Navajo Nation

Peter MacDonald was first elected chairman of the Navajo Nation in 1970 on a strong self-determination platform that resonated deeply among the people who had stood by and witnessed the horrific destruction caused by strip mining and coal-fired power plants. In an effort to bring much-needed jobs and find tribal revenues, the previous tribal council had signed a contract in 1962 with Utah Mining and Manufacturing, which proceeded to strip-mine coal from the area south of the San Juan River. In 1964 and 1966, the tribal council also leased lands on Black Mesa to the Peabody Coal Company and permitted another power plant to be built (one had already been constructed by the Arizona Public Service Company). The Navajos could not have foreseen the destruction of land that resulted. "Huge steam-powered shovel machines called draglines, as tall as sixteen-story buildings, weighing 27 million pounds and able to move 220 cubic yards (325 tons) of 'overburden'—earth—in a single pass" leave an enormous miles-wide gouge in the earth after the strip-mining process.[56] Precious water resources were contaminated as well. The pollution produced by coal-burning plants threatened the health of the people as well as their livestock and threatened tourism that had provided a steady, if small, source of revenue.

At the time that MacDonald challenged Raymond Nakai in the general tribal elections, many Navajo people were also upset by the loss of what had long been established as joint-use lands with neighboring Hopi people. A court decision awarding the Hopis exclusive rights ensured MacDonald's three-to-one election victory over Nakai.[57]

MacDonald's administration achieved some early success: Under his leadership, the tribal council formed a Navajo Division of Education and increased the number of Navajo teachers; the Navajo Housing Authority was organized; and most importantly, MacDonald renegotiated gas and oil leases, securing better terms for the Navajos for the use of their land. At the same time, he permitted Exxon to begin uranium exploration on tribal lands in northwestern New Mexico. Those Navajos living in that area protested, concerned about the health of Navajo miners, as well as that of everyone living in the vicinity. The 1979 Three Mile Island nuclear power plant incident in Pennsylvania only heightened their fears. Later that year, this country's worst accident with radioactive material came about when United Nuclear Corporation's uranium tailings dam failed at Church Rock, just off the Navajo Reservation. One hundred million gallons of radioactive water flooded the Rio Puerco, resulting in the death of ten thousand sheep.[58]

The creation of the Navajo Forest Products Industries and the Navajo Agricultural Products Industry fulfilled MacDonald's promise to bring new jobs to the reservation that would be placed under tribal control. In addition, some new small businesses owned and operated by Navajos opened. Thus MacDonald, in his first term, "appeared to provide bold new leadership for the Navajos. He challenged them to raise their ambitions and to develop a more assertive posture . . . He outlined goals for the future and projected confidence that the people could meet these goals."[59]

A controversial figure among today's American Indians is former Navajo Tribal Chairman Peter MacDonald, who is seen here with then-President Richard Nixon in 1970. During his run as tribal chairman, MacDonald helped promote self-reliance among his people, but he ended up being sentenced to fourteen years in federal prison for racketeering charges and accepting kickbacks and bribes from the corporations he did business with.

MacDonald was reelected for a second term as tribal chairman by a comfortable margin. But he also acquired increasing numbers of critics who accused him of cozying up too much to the energy companies. His role in helping to bring twenty tribal groups together to form the Council of Energy Resource Tribes (CERT) in 1975, as well as his charming personality, projected him onto a national stage. Increasingly, he looked as though he belonged more in a corporate boardroom than at the helm of an Indian nation—an image further tarnished in 1977 when he was indicted by a Phoenix, Arizona, grand jury on eight counts of fraud, even though the jury was unable to reach a verdict in the trial that followed.[60] Nonetheless, MacDonald was elected for an unprecedented third term in 1978.

Concerns about MacDonald's land-use policies, combined with the skills of Peterson Zah, director of the DNA (*Dinebeiina Nahiilna be Agitahe*—the Navajo Nation's legal defense service), persuaded the Navajos to elect Zah to the chairmanship in 1982. Unfortunately, Zah's chairmanship began at precisely the time when the cutbacks to domestic programs made by the Reagan administration began to be felt most sharply throughout Indian Country. His inability to prevent Navajos living on lands awarded to the Hopis from being relocated also led to increased criticism.

In 1986, MacDonald was elected once again as chairman in a very close race. His determination to hold onto power this time became apparent as he tried to silence the tribal newspaper, the *Navajo Times*, which had been a steady critic of MacDonald's policies. Still worse, in January 1979, he was accused during hearings of the U.S. Senate Select Committee on Indian Affairs of taking kickbacks from corporate interests; that is, he was profiting personally from using tribal funds. MacDonald admitted during an interview on KTNN Radio, a station in Window Rock, Arizona, that he had taken "gifts" in order to secure business deals. "Yes I have accepted gifts," he said. "But that is not a crime."[61]

This admission divided the Navajos into two factions—one pro- and one anti-MacDonald. Both claimed control over tribal government. The tribal council placed MacDonald on administrative leave and appointed an interim chairman. But the struggle for power continued, leading to an eruption of violence in July 1989 when two Navajo men were killed and others injured in a confrontation between MacDonald's supporters and the Navajo tribal police.

Such violence is rare on the reservation but the struggle for power between competing factions produced a similar incident on the Seneca Cattaraugus Reservation in 1997, during which three Seneca men died. Some of the most fractious political debates in recent years have taken place in the Cherokee capital of Tahlequah, as different groups within the tribe struggled for control.

Unity through Reform

To try and promote unity, Indian nations employ different measures. Some write and/or rewrite their constitutions to give greater voice to all. "That's one of the things that people always talk about is having more representation," explains Nathan Hale, cochairman of the committee to revise the constitution of the Three Affiliated Tribes: the Mandan, Hidatsa and Arikara people.[62] Under their new constitution, the legislature or council will have fourteen members, including the chairman, replacing the present six-person council. Each district will now be represented.

Without a doubt, continuing intratribal factionalism undermines sovereignty. But such infighting is part of the nature of politics in any culture. For Indian people, the stakes are high, however. Their continuing trustee relationship with the federal government, which is handled primarily through the BIA, and the greed of state as well as corporate officials for Indian land and resources means that the tribe must come together to meet the threat facing them all. Indian peoples recognize this. And the danger is very real. Today the Navajo Nation is united in its efforts to fight the resumption of uranium mining in the same area already once polluted by a radioactive spill. The new mining operations, which are under consideration of the Nuclear Regulatory Commission, has the potential to contaminate the drinking water of fifteen thousand Navajos. A groundwater hydrologist who has examined the site condemns the U.S. government's hearings: "I've never seen such poor science, poor accountability and poor traceability."[63]

Creating a schism among tribal members seems to be the goal of some state governments, which seek to obtain what they want by promoting that division. Issues of land settlements and casino gambling come to the forefront to divide Indian groups. In 2004, New York governor George Pataki signed an agreement with the St. Regis Mohawk Tribe, the antigambling Mohawk Nation Council of Chiefs, and the Mohawk Council of Akwesasne (representing Mohawks north of the Canadian border). Other Mohawks oppose this deal, running ads in local newspapers urging the twenty thousand Mohawk tribal members to vote no and reject the settlement. The Ganienkeh group charged that "the three Mohawk groups who signed it had no authority to do so."[64]

Their protest echoes those made by Dragging Canoe in challenging the authority of the Cherokee chiefs who signed away tribal land in the eighteenth century, the actions taken by the Creek Tribal Council in punishing William McIntosh for ceding lands in violation of Council decision, and the actions of countless "government chiefs" who have been used throughout American history to gain Indian land and resources. The 1975 Indian Self-Determination Act returned authority for home rule to the Indian nations. It is up to the nations now to answer the question: Who rules at home? Disputes will, no doubt, continue as they do in every culture. But unity is necessary to protect tribal sovereignty and enable Indian peoples to develop the real economic and political infrastructure necessary to achieve true self-determination.

6

Federal Trustee Status

In 1824, Congress created the Bureau of Indian Affairs (BIA) under the direction of John C. Calhoun, then secretary of war. Twenty-five years later, the bureau was transferred to the newly established Department of the Interior, where it was intended to act as the agency principally responsible for all Indian affairs.

The responsibility of the U.S. government to treat Indian nations fairly, that is, "with the utmost good faith" had been laid out in the Northwest Ordinance of 1787. Implicit recognition of tribal sovereignty was expressed in the Marshall Court's *Cherokee Nation v. Georgia* decision, in 1831, defining Indian peoples as "domestic dependent nations." But federal recognition of Indian sovereignty came to an abrupt halt in 1871, when a rider was added to the Indian appropriation bill, ending federal practice of using treaty negotiation:

Provided: That hereafter no Indian nation or tribe within the territory of the United States shall be acknowledged or recognized as an independent nation, tribe, or power with whom the United States may contract by treaty: *Provided Further*, That nothing herein contained shall be construed to invalidate or impair the obligation of any treaty heretofore lawfully made and ratified with any such Indian nation or tribe. . . .[65]

THE FEDERAL GOVERNMENT AS TRUSTEE

After 1871, Indian nations were not to be considered sovereign nations, although the promises made through previous treaties and U.S. laws were still being enforced and the federal government promised they would be upheld. In other words, Indian peoples now became wards of the federal government, which, in its trustee capacity, would be responsible for their welfare. That chore fell principally to the BIA. As a result, the bureau grew quickly into an unwieldy hodgepodge of administrators, some responsible for the operation of Indian agencies, others undertaking the establishment of Indian schools for the education and acculturation of the next generation, still others dealing with land-use policies with emphasis on promoting irrigation and agriculture projects on western reservations. Most of these issues came together following the passage of the General Allotment Act in 1887, with its emphasis on enforced acculturation through the destruction of reservations and tribal governments.

There remained the problem of providing law and order on the reservations. In the late 1870s, BIA agents began the organization of Indian police forces. On March 3, 1885, Congress passed the Seven *Major Crimes Act* extending federal jurisdiction to Indian Country. In effect, this law "precluded any tribes (except the "Five Civilized Tribes") from exercising criminal jurisdiction over crimes of a serious nature."[66] This outlawing of tribal councils from exercising traditional means of dealing with those who violated the peace became even stronger with the passage of the Assimilative Crimes Act of 1898. Essentially this was a "catchall" bill, designed to make criminal offenses not covered under federal penal codes—but that violated state laws—subject to federal criminal prosecution. The "Five Civilized Tribes"—the Cherokee, Chickasaw, Choctaw, Creek, and Seminole in Oklahoma Territory—did not remain exempt for long. The Curtis Act of 1898 banned tribal courts and declared that tribal laws would carry no weight in federal courts. Not until 1970 would the "Five Civilized Tribes" regain the right to elect their tribal leaders.[67]

Most tribal governments throughout the country continued to try and exert a measure of rule over their own people. Distracted by what the BIA viewed as larger issues of acculturation, land use, and education, the BIA permitted the tribes to, more or less, handle domestic disputes, interfering only in those crimes "of a serious nature" in adherence to the Major Crimes Act. The Indian Reorganization Act of 1934 restored tribal government and courts to those nations that opted to accept its provisions. Tribal referenda were organized on the reservations to examine the IRA. One hundred eighty-nine tribes voted to accept it with 135 Indian communities drafting constitutions, but 77 rejected the IRA, viewing it as only another BIA policy mandate, one that did not include the true self-determination provisions that activists, many of them former members of the Society of American Indians, demanded.[68]

Nonetheless, federal recognition of inherent tribal sovereignty was laid out by one of Collier's attorneys, Felix S. Cohen, in his 1942 *Handbook of Federal Indian Law*:

> Perhaps the most basic principle of all Indian law, supported by a host of decisions . . . is the principle that *those powers which are lawfully vested in Indian tribes are not, in general, delegated powers granted by express acts of Congress but rather inherent powers of a limited sovereignty, which has never been*

extinguished. Each Indian tribe begins its relationship with the Federal Government as a sovereign power, recognized as such in treaty and legislation. The powers of sovereignty have been limited from time to time by special treaties and laws designed to take from the Indian tribes control of matters which, in the judgment of Congress, these tribes could no longer be safely permitted to handle. The statutes of Congress, then, must be examined to determine the limitations of tribal sovereignty . . . What is not expressly limited remains within the domain of tribal sovereignty.[69]

Limited Sovereignty

The key phrase in the aforementioned excerpt is "limited sovereignty." The Indian Self-Determination Act passed by Congress in 1975 restored some measure of home rule to Indian tribes, bands, and communities but the power of the federal government to impose boundaries on this concept of self-rule was laid out in the Supreme Court case *United States v. Wheeler* three years later. Full sovereignty, the Court ruled, no longer existed. Rather Congress had the right, indeed the obligation, to exercise "plenary control," as established through a long history of treaties and Indian policy laws. In other words, Indian tribes may be self-governing but only with Congress (and by extension the BIA) acting as a Big Brother, always watching with full power to interfere at any time.[70] Indeed, that is the meaning of *plenary control*: that ultimate power lies with the federal government and not with the tribes.

One power immediately restricted was the power of Indian tribal courts to deal with crimes committed by non-Indians on the reservation. Judicial precedent was set in *Oliphant v. Suquamish Indian Tribe.* Mark Oliphant, a non-Indian, was living on the Port Madison Reservation in Washington State when he was arrested for assaulting a tribal officer. He appealed on the grounds that he was not subject to tribal authority and won his case.[71] Judge William Rehnquist wrote the Supreme Court's majority opinion, undermining tribal authority over crimes committed by non-Indians on the reservations.

The principle that non-Indians living on the reservation were not bound to obey tribal law was further upheld in 1981 in *Montana v. United States*. Here, the Supreme Court held that the Crow tribe could not regulate hunting and fishing by those who were not tribal members on fee title lands held by non-Indians. Even on the reservation, the Supreme Court ruled, "inherent sovereign powers of an Indian tribe do not extend to the activities of nonmembers of the tribe."[72] The Rehnquist Court reinforced this principle the following year, ruling that Indian courts did not have criminal jurisdiction over an Indian who was not a member of the tribe on whose land the crime had been committed.[73] This time, however, the Supreme Court had gone too far and Congress passed legislation the following year upholding the power of the tribes to enforce their laws over all Indians on the reservation, whether the person charged with committing a crime was a tribal member or not.

The BIA operates a training academy for Indian police officers, as does the Navajo Nation. However, the pendulum of federal Indian policy has swung again away from the civil rights culture of the 1960s and 1970s that produced legislation so important in returning responsibilities for self-rule to Indian peoples. The Supreme Court under Chief Justice Berger (1969–1985) ruled in favor of Indians in 58 percent of the cases it accepted for consideration. By contrast, the Rehnquist Court has reversed that tide, ruling against Indian people 77 percent of the time during the years 1986 to 2001.[74] Indeed, Chief Justice Rehnquist reveals both his scorn for and ignorance of Indian law in his statement that "few Indian tribes maintained any semblance of a formal court system . . . offenses by one Indian against another were usually handled by social and religious pressure and not by formal judicial processes; emphasis was on restitution rather than punishment."[75]

The chief justice is correct in his assessment that Indian courts would prefer to find means of reconciliation rather than impose punishments. This approach is in keeping with traditional Indian practices. Before American reformers and policy makers began imposing non-Indian styles of courts on the tribes, Indian nations, for the most part, found the means of jurisprudence that would enable people who made mistakes, that is, committed crimes, to compensate those they had wronged. Again, religion and ritual provided the steps by which an offender could cleanse himself of his evil act and take his place once again among the people. It was a highly workable system, one in which the death penalty was virtually unknown. Instead, banishment was imposed on those who could not be reconciled to the community. Today, many Indian governments still employ peacekeepers to try and work out disputes. Part of the reason lies in an adherence to traditional practice, which is followed not only because of its cultural heritage but because it still seems to be the most sensible way of dealing with disagreements that are always going to arise in any community.

Moreover, few Indian nations have the ready cash to build adequate jail facilities. In December 2004, for example, the Yakama tribal jail in Washington State came under federal investigation because of the attempted suicide of a 17-year-old boy who was being held there in violation of a BIA directive that juveniles could not be incarcerated along with adults. Fortunately the boy survived, but the FBI has also entered the investigation. Tribal Council Vice Chairman Virgil Lewis reported that the tribe had attempted to cooperate with county authorities that have the facilities to house juvenile offenders but could come to no agreement because of the costs involved. The tribe is currently seeking a way to ensure that future teenagers who are arrested will be detained in places of safety. In the meantime, they must also worry that incidents like this provide the BIA with an excuse to take over operation of the jail—another infringement on tribal sovereignty.[76]

The Ineffectual BIA

Many Indian peoples have long been wary of the Bureau of Indian Affairs. There are undoubtedly many decent and dedicated people who work within the bureau, some of whom are Indian. Indeed, in the wake of the 1975 Indian Self-Determination Act, preferential consideration is given to tribal members when staffing BIA agencies on the reservation. But the bureau in Washington, D.C., has always been the focal point of a storm of controversy. It was the BIA, after all, that enforced the Dawes Commissioners' allotment of Indian reservations into individual holdings and destroyed tribal governments. It was BIA agents who carried out John Collier's orders during the Depression Era to destroy Navajo sheep, ostensibly to prevent over-grazing, but they instead ran roughshod over both tribal council and individual Navajo families, slaughtering whole herds by the thousands.

Carlos Montezuma attempted to rally Indian peoples against the BIA in the 1920s with the publication of *Wassaja*, and its slogan, "Let my People Go." Other Indian activists resisted BIA hegemony over Indian affairs for reasons that often differed from Montezuma's objections, but all saw the bureau as an impediment to Indian self-determination.

In 1869, President Ulysses S. Grant appointed his former adjutant, Ely Parker, to become commissioner of Indian affairs, the first Indian to hold the post.[77] Parker served as head of the BIA until 1871, when a House of Representatives committee brought charges of incompetence against him and forced his resignation.[78] This strategy to try and defer criticism by appointing an Indian to head the BIA has been repeated in recent years. During his first term, President George W. Bush named Dave Anderson, an enrolled member of the Lac Courte Oreilles band of Ojibwe in Wisconsin to head the BIA. Anderson is a talented businessman and a widely respected Ojibwe community leader, but he decided to resign in February 2005. And it will take more than the talents of one man to pull the BIA out of the mire of scandal, incompetence, and corruption into which it has fallen.

The most long-standing issue facing the BIA is the Indian Trust fund. For more than a century, the bureau managed billions of dollars gained from grazing, mineral, and timber leases plus oil and gas payments, as well as the outright sale of Indian lands under the terms of the General Allotment Act. So where is the money? What happened to all those funds that the BIA was managing under the general assumption that Indian peoples were incapable of doing so? Little wonder that a common joke heard in Indian Country is that BIA actually stands for "Billions in Invisible Assets."[79]

The Indian Health Service, which is obligated by numerous treaties to provide medical treatment for Indian peoples, is underfunded, short-staffed, and must make do with often less than adequate equipment. Many foreign students work off the enormous loans they incur to make their way through medical school at reservation IHS clinics. The resulting variety of accents often make communication between doctor and patient difficult, especially among those Indian peoples for whom English is not necessarily their first language. Indian Health Services do not apply to the vast majority of Indian peoples who, although they may be enrolled tribal members and recognized by the BIA as Indian, live away from the reservation. In any event, medical care in many of the reservation clinics is so poor that one recent writer to H-AmIndian, which is an e-mail forum run by Arizona State University for those interested in the histories and cultures of North American Indians, described it as "just about as hazardous to my health as my similar entitlement to use the Veterans Administration."[80] As a result, life expectancy for Indian peoples remains about twenty years shorter than for Anglo American peoples.

The BIA's Web site has remained offline for more than three years as of this writing because of a continuing controversy surrounding security flaws that permitted access to trust account

Former Colorado Senator Ben Nighthorse Campbell (Northern Cheyenne), who served as chairman of the Committee on Indian Affairs during the 105th and 106th Congress, has been critical of the policies of the Bureau of Indian Affairs and has long tried to change the way the BIA recognizes tribes.

data. No other U.S. government agency has remained offline for so long, a situation directly related to demands for BIA accountability over what happened to the billions of dollars in missing funds that belong to Indian peoples.

Because of their unique status as nations within a nation, Indian peoples must continue to work with the BIA, which tries to act as a facilitator in identifying which Indian groups are deserving of federal recognition, which individuals may receive a CDIB card identifying them as Indian, and in coordinating tribal applications for Indian Health and education services, and so forth. But the scandals remain, leading many today to echo Carlos Montezuma's call nearly a century ago for the BIA's abolition. Ben Nighthorse Campbell, the outgoing Cheyenne senator from Colorado who retired in 2005, sums up the situation at the BIA: "There seems to be an institutional rot that does not seem to go away."[81]

The Native American Rights Fund

Today, Indian peoples must seek recourse through Congress and the courts for issues involving reclamation of land, restoration of rights stolen during the Termination Era, protection of tribal self-government against infringements from the states, and other problems that surround the protection of sovereignty, even if it is limited sovereignty. This situation has become increasingly difficult over the last twenty years as the federal courts have proven themselves not particularly sympathetic to Indian law or self-rule.

To meet these challenges of the modern era, the *Native American Rights Fund*, a nonprofit organization formed in 1970, has brought together attorneys who specialize in Indian law. Its self-defined mission is to provide legal representation and assistance to Indian groups and individuals. Its specific goals as outlined in its mission statement:

- Preservation of tribal existence
- Protection of tribal natural resources
- Promotion of Native American human rights
- Accountability of governments to Native Americans
- Development of Indian law and educating the public about Indian rights, laws, and issues.[82]

To achieve these goals, NARF provides expertise to help formulate legislation to promote Indian rights. But it serves primarily to prosecute or defend Indian entitlement cases in the courts. It will only accept cases based on issues involving attempted infringement on Indian rights—either tribal or individual—but it will not assist Indian people who seek to bring suit against other Indians. In other words, NARF plays no role in furthering the already serious problem of tribal factionalism.

Over the years, NARF has achieved many notable successes. It was active in representing the Passamaquoddys and Penobscots of Maine to regain part of their lands taken from them and to receive restitution ($81.5 million) for other stolen property, ultimately resulting in the Maine Indian Claims Settlement Act of 1980—the largest return of Indian lands to the tribes in U.S. history. NARF has also provided the necessary legal assistance to a number of tribes that enabled them to win federal recognition.

NARF has provided legal assistance to tribes to protect Indian hunting and fishing rights guaranteed to them by treaty against corporate, state, sportsmen, and sometimes even federal agencies. In the West, water is often the most valuable resource. The Winters Doctrine, laid down by the Supreme Court in 1908, guaranteed prior appropriation rights of Indian people to have first use claim on water. The rights were further defined when the Supreme Court ruled in *Arizona v. California* (1963) that Indian water rights were preeminent over other claimants and that the amount of water reserved for Indian first use should be determined by the amount necessary to irrigate the entire reservation.[83] In the 1970s, NARF was successful in achieving favorable court decisions upholding these water rights, enabling Indian tribes throughout the West to have sufficient resources to develop their own industries.

The shifting of political winds throughout the federal government in the 1980s to the present means that NARF has faced increasing challenges. The Supreme Court, in particular, tends to rule against Indian people, returning cases to the state courts for decision. This has happened so often that some Indian activists charge that the Rehnquist Court seems determined to bring about a new era of Termination policy.

Indian peoples are well aware of the challenges facing them in today's era of a federal government that, in Indian eyes, seems determined to abandon them once again to the states. The

Why Should You Vote?

One of the goals of early Pan-Indian organizations, such as the National Council of American Indians, was to try and urge Indian peoples to use their votes (a right extended to all by the 1924 Indian Citizenship Act) to influence elections. Today, Indian sovereignty—their right to exist as nations within a larger nation—is under attack. Tribal governments are well aware of the danger posed by politicians who seek to turn back the clock to the years of Termination. At the same time, they seek to endorse those candidates who pledge themselves to protecting treaty promises. One example of this effort to encourage Indian people to vote comes from Cherokee Nation chief Chad Smith, who submitted a letter to the nation's newspaper, prior to the 2004 Senate election in Oklahoma. The letter was titled: "Why You Should Vote":

> Today, we are faced with anti-Indian hate groups and several candidates, including U.S. Senate candidate Tom Coburn repeating the same outdated slogan that the Cherokee Nation cannot be a "sovereign within a sovereign" . . . history's lessons are undeniable. Every 20 [to] 40 years, public sentiment and federal policy goes against the Cherokee Nation and other tribes. Now, instead of historical policies of genocide, removal, ethnocide, assimilation, extortion, allotment, dissolution and relocation, the federal policy could shift towards abandonment. These groups and their candidates do not believe in federal programs, tribal sovereignty and gaming . . .
>
> Candidates like Coburn are not only against our self-sufficiency and the U.S. government. They seek to nullify the right guaranteed in our 23 treaties with Great Britain and the United States. . . . We cannot allow Coburn to follow in the footsteps of Andrew Jackson and Senator Dawes, who did everything they could to destroy the Cherokee Nation. . . . Each of us will make history and decide the future of the Cherokee Nation on November 2, 2004.*

Despite Smith's passionate message to his people, Coburn garnered nearly 53 percent of the vote and defeated former Oklahoma congressman and Cherokee Nation member Brad Carson to claim the senate seat.

* Full text of Chief Smith's letter can be accessed at *www.cherokee.org/NewsArchives /Announcements/VoterGuide.asp*

Peter Pino (left), governor of Zia Pueblo, recognizes the importance of the American Indian vote for both Republicans and Democrats—states in the Midwest and West have higher Native populations and thus their votes are courted by those running for office. In March 2004, President George W. Bush met with ten of the nineteen Pueblo governors in Albuquerque, New Mexico, including Pino.

response of many nations has been to organize tribal members to vote. Prior to the 2004 elections, for example, the Cherokee Nation posted on its Web site evaluations of each candidate and referendum issue, urging its members to turn out and vote.[84] The stakes could not be higher. The U.S. Senate must approve all presidential appointments to the federal courts. If there is any hope of restoring concern for Indian welfare among the courts, Indian peoples must use their power as voting blocs to ensure fair-minded candidates are elected to Congress. Also at issue are Congress' *plenary powers* over the tribes. Will treaties be upheld or not? Will prior Supreme Court decisions honoring those treaty obligations be allowed to stand?

Indian nations also watch the presidential elections closely. In 2004, both Republican and Democratic organizers worked throughout Indian Country to court the Indian vote. "It feels good, because people are starting to fight over our vote, and we feel like we can make a difference," stated Peter Pino, governor of Zia Pueblo, in September 2004. Comanche activist LaDonna Harris supports that view, noting that although Indians comprise only 1.5 percent of the overall population, their numbers in some Midwestern and Western states make them a much larger proportion of the electorate. "Our numbers are small, but we tend to vote as a block."[85] For example, the Navajos and other American Indians represent 19 percent of Arizona's eligible voters, sufficient numbers to swing an election one way or the other.

Indian voter participation is vital to electing members to Congress who will honorably uphold the obligations of their trustee relationship to the tribes. In the Supreme Court's landmark 1831 decision in *Cherokee Nation v. Georgia*, Chief Justice John Marshall introduced the famous phrase that described Indian tribes as "domestic dependent nations." Domestic because they exist within the boundaries of the United States; they are nations within a nation. Dependent because they are minority citizens of the United States and therefore must rely upon the goodwill of the majority. And finally nation, which underscores the sovereignty of Indian tribes. As was the case in 1831, this continuing sovereignty is challenged primarily by the states. It is the responsibility of the federal government to fulfill its trustee obligations. The "utmost good faith" with which Congress promised to treat Indian peoples in the Northwest Ordinance of 1787 is of vital importance today if Indian nations are going to be successful in resisting attempted state inroads against their lands, resources, industries—and sovereignty.

7

Sovereignty versus
the States

M any public opinion surveys exist to show that the majority of
U.S. citizens are perfectly willing to acknowledge, often in highly
romanticized accounts, the sovereignty of Indian peoples that existed
for thousands of years prior to European contact. Most Americans
are proud of Indian history but only on terms they define, fitting it
into an overall perception of national identity. Indians are part of
U.S. distinctiveness, the myth of our cultural heritage, and within
those parameters, Americans never hesitate to lay claim to Indian
symbols, using them for everything from sports teams—the Atlanta
Braves, the Washington Redskins, the Florida State Seminoles, and so
on—to selling Red Man Chewing Tobacco that features a sketch of a
Plains Indian war chief on its wrapping.

THE RIGHT TO SOVEREIGNTY
Undoubtedly, many sports fans, advertisers, consumers, and so on

Many products available in stores today use names, images, and symbols that inaccurately represent Native American culture. Such notable American Indians as Geronimo and Crazy Horse have had their name and images used to promote consumer goods. Shown here is Judy Dow, who visits schools to raise awareness about the misrepresentation of Native Americans.

see no problem in using Indian images as a way to promote sports teams and products. Indians are, after all, part of the American past. Indians in the present are another question. Non-Indian America appears to be largely ignorant of the laws, treaties, and judicial case precedents that uphold the rights of Indian tribes and bands to be self-governing, that is, to exist as sovereign entities outside the control of state and local municipalities. This ignorance most often appears over the question of taxes. As is implicit in their sovereign status, Indian peoples earning money within Indian Country are not subject to state taxes—income, sales, or property. Many people see no reason why Indians should not pay taxes to the states and counties in which they reside. A poll released in January 2005 revealed that three-quarters of all likely voters in Madison and Oneida counties in central New York believe that local officials should tax the members of the Oneida Nation. The poll goes on to reveal that these people believe the Oneidas are using their sovereignty to "illegally avoid paying taxes and create an unfair advantage for Oneida-owned businesses."[86]

For people living in the "Rust Belt" of the Midwest (stretching from central New York, westward, where factory closures have produced high unemployment rates), the argument that Indians should be treated no differently from any other American resonates strongly. But it flies in the face not only of the laws guaranteeing the rights of Indians to exist as sovereign nations but also the economic reality that Indian businesses often serve to provide jobs for non-Indians living in proximity to the reservations. In Mississippi, for example, Choctaw businesses have created fifteen thousand permanent jobs, many of them held by non-Indian peoples, which has resulted in a $357 million payroll for Mississippi workers, and generated $20 million in state tax revenues. Indeed, the Mississippi Choctaws are today the second-largest employer in the state. Yet Mississippi, like other states, seeks to take more from its Indian people. Tribal Chairman Phillip Martin has attempted to defend his band's sovereignty, citing a survey by Mississippi State University that outlines the already substantial Choctaw contribution to the state economy: "Some people complain that we don't pay [state] taxes, but they fail to acknowledge that we do not cost the state anything either . . . This study by Mississippi State University shows that we are a huge financial benefit for Mississippi, and we don't ask for anything in return."[87]

Sovereignty Challenged by States

In many ways, the current struggle between Indian nations and the states continues the adversarial stance that has existed since the first English colonies along the Atlantic seaboard were settled. Those colonies made treaties with their Indian neighbors, always with an eye to gaining their land. Some states later used the same process, making treaties with their Indian peoples even after the Constitution reserved that right solely to the federal government. One example is the Buffalo Creek Treaty of 1842 in which the State of New York promised to respect and not tax Indian lands; although this treaty has not stopped the current government in Albany from trying to infringe on those rights. Similarly in the 1820s and 1830s, it was the State of Georgia that, particularly after the discovery of gold on Cherokee land near Dahlonega, wanted to push the Cherokees out. To accomplish that end, they helped elect well-known Indian fighter Andrew Jackson to the presidency in 1828. Jackson sided with the state. The Supreme Court did not, leading to Marshall's famous *Cherokee Nation v. Georgia* decision, defining Indian peoples as "domestic, dependant nations."[88]

After World War II, it was state greed for Indian lands that prompted Congress to initiate Termination, uprooting thousands of Indians from their homes and dumping them in cities, with the promise of helping them find new employment—guarantees that proved to be mere words. Meanwhile, Indian lands were taken away, their businesses destroyed, and their extended families separated.

The suspension (but not retraction) of Termination in the early 1970s interrupted state seizure of Indian properties. In fact, it was the states, early proponents of Termination, that soon came to call for its end. The destruction of tribal sovereignty and economies placed too many people on state welfare rolls. Since that time, agencies such as the Native American Rights Fund (NARF) have provided legal assistance to try and reclaim lands lost under Termination. They achieved significant progress in some instances, most notably among the Menominees of Wisconsin, when on April 23, 1975, the Menominee Indian Reservation was formally restored as a federally recognized and sovereign tribe.[89]

In the last two decades, the Supreme Court, as well as federal district courts, have proven to be far less amenable to upholding Indian rights. In 2003, for example, New Mexico collected state income taxes on salaries owed to Pueblo soldiers living on the reservation. When these veterans brought suit, the federal court refused to hear the case. This practice of abrogating federal responsibilities by returning cases to the courts to decide was made clear in 1983 when the Supreme Court overturned a lower court's decision to set aside sufficient water to enable the Pyramid Lake Paiutes to operate their fishery. In *Arizona v. San Carlos Apache Tribe*, the Court stated "that old water allocations were void and that state courts should decide future ones."[90]

This increasing reluctance of the federal courts to fulfill long-standing responsibilities of trusteeship and protect Indian nations against state inroads amounts to a threatened return to Termination in fact, if not in law. And Indian peoples have good reason to fear the states, their long-time adversaries. Even after the 1924 Indian Citizenship Act, many states, especially in the West, imposed Jim Crow laws, effectively barring Indian peoples from the polls. Even in the East, racial prejudice against Indian peoples remained manifest. In Virginia, for example, it was illegal throughout the 1950s for anyone to declare him/herself to be Indian on a birth certificate.[91]

The 1975 Indian Self-Determination Act, in conjunction with the 1974 Indian Financing Act, enabled some tribes and bands to begin operating businesses in order to provide needed income for their people. In some cases, the Indian nations have achieved considerable success using a variety of strategies. One of the first proven fiscally viable operations opened were small shops where fuel and cigarettes could be sold at rates lower than could be found off the reservation, because sales taxes were not applied. Many states have attempted to bring pressure to bear to collect those taxes. Unable under federal law to tax those sales directly, the states have pursued other means, primarily by applying extra charges to non-Indian companies that supply the reservation shops with their gas. In a case involving the Prairie Band Potawatomi Nation in Kansas, the Denver-based United States Court of Appeals for the Tenth Circuit ruled that this tax on wholesalers violated tribal sovereignty and also interfered with interstate commerce in violation of the Constitution.

Kansas has appealed with the support of thirteen other states that also seek to reap benefits from the reservation fuel sales. These states—Arizona, California, Connecticut, Idaho, Iowa, Massachusetts, Missouri, New Mexico, North Dakota, Oklahoma, South Dakota, Utah, and Wyoming—have filed friend of the court briefs. In February 2005, the Supreme Court agreed to hear the case even though the infringement on Indian sovereignty and violation of congressional and constitutional guarantees seem clear.[92]

The Senecas and New York

State police officers are not permitted to enter a reservation without the permission of tribal council or whatever governance the Indian peoples on that reservation choose for their leadership. Nonetheless, the state can find other ways to bring pressure to bear. One example occurred in New York in 1997. Under the Buffalo Creek Treaty of 1842, New York guaranteed not to apply taxes on Seneca land. But Governor George Pataki seems determined to collect revenues from Indian people in defiance of both federal and state treaties, as well as Congress'

In 1997, New York Governor George Pataki set out to levy a state tax on tobacco products that the Senecas sold in reservation smoke shops. After the Senecas refused to comply, the governor ordered New York State Police to block the roads (shown here) that led out of the Cattaraugus Reservation. Fortunately, the standoff only lasted a few days, but the proposed tax remains a point of contention.

plenary rights. When the Senecas refused to submit to state taxation, citing both state and federal treaty guarantees, the governor ordered state troopers to surround the Cattaraugus Reservation. The New York State Police did not enter the reservation but they closed every road, permitting no one of Indian blood to leave. Still worse, nothing was permitted to be brought onto the reservation—no fuel, no groceries, nothing. Like many reservations, Cattaraugus has no grocery stores. People travel to nearby towns to do their shopping. Moreover, this entrapment happened in April and spring comes late in that part of the country. It was still quite cold and many people did not have adequate fuel supplies on hand to heat their homes while the siege continued.

Everyone shared what they had and eventually public pressure forced the governor to withdraw the state troopers, most of whom didn't want to be there in the first place, scornfully calling this event, "Pataki's War."[93] When we could again leave the reservation, we saw that surrounding residents had tried to help, putting up homemade signs in their yards with boldly painted slogans, which most commonly read: "Leave our Indians alone." Some may charge that our non-Indian neighbors only wanted to maintain their access to cheap gas and cigarettes. But they also displayed genuine outrage at this flagrant abuse of state power.

Governor Pataki has continued to insist that the state has the right to collect sales taxes on all purchases made by non-Indian people at reservation businesses. He ignores the contribution already made by Seneca people to the surrounding economy—the Senecas must spend their money off the reservation for all retail purchases, from food to clothing to automobiles.

In an effort to circumvent the governor's determination to collect state sales taxes, the Senecas turned to the Internet to sell tobacco, a move that defied a 2000 state law banning such sales. But the Senecas had little choice after the New York State Department of Taxation and Finance announced that it would collect the $1.50 state tax on each pack of cigarettes from suppliers before they could deliver to reservation stores. The Internet sales brought needed revenues to the reservation, providing jobs to 1,500 people. The U.S. District Court rejected the suit brought by the Senecas to challenge the Internet ban. In March 2005, the major credit card companies announced they would no longer permit their cards to be used to pay for Internet sales of tobacco, using the justification that such sales interfered with the state's ability to collect revenues. In fact, this is a big blow to Indian tobacco shops nationwide, which tried to avoid confrontation with the state tax collector.

In some states, Indian peoples have tried to compromise with state officials before the troopers are sent to surround them, as happened in New York. In 2003, the Coeur d'Alene, along with Idaho's other three major Indian tribes, announced they would add tax stamps to all cigarettes sold on the reservation.

The Senecas choose to continue to resist, primarily through a media campaign called "Honor Indian Treaties," which seeks to raise awareness of the issue.[94] In the end, however, the Senecas, like so many other Indian peoples, will be forced to turn to casino gambling to provide jobs for its tribal members. The Seneca Niagara Casino opened on New Year's Eve 2003, followed by the Seneca Allegany Casino (in Salamanca), which began operations in May 2004.[95] Considerable dissent continues to exist among the Senecas over the use of gambling. The resulting factionalism provides yet another issue that divides the people, setting one group against another. Such infighting plays right into the states' hands and undermines sovereignty.

Gaming: Should States Get a Piece of the Pie?

Undoubtedly, the building of casinos has played a preeminent role in boosting tribal economies and thus the self-sufficiency needed to maintain sovereignty. The most successful example is the aforementioned Mashantucket Pequots' Foxwoods Casino in Ledyard, Connecticut, which boasts that it is the largest gaming operation in the world. Certainly, the casino generates enormous revenues that the Pequots have used to provide jobs for their people. They have gone further, donating money to scholarships and other needed endowments to serve the greater good. Revenues from the Foxwood Casino made possible the building of a $193 million museum and library collection. The museum exists to educate Pequot children about their heritage but also seeks to inform the public at large. "We want to show that Native peoples are not a static part of history, but are still evolving, vital contributors to modern society," explained David Holahan, a Pequot spokesman. "We will show that Native peoples may not be what the public often expects or envisions them to be. That's part of the learning process."[96]

Other nations have opened casinos as well. In 1998, Indian gaming reported revenues of $500 million. By 2002, 290 Indian casinos cited a combined profit of $12.7 billion.[97] Such outstanding success was, of course, going to attract the attention of the states that want a share of these funds.

In 1988, Congress passed the *Indian Gaming Regulatory Act*, establishing the *National Indian Gaming Commission* (NIGC) and regulating how Indian tribes must work with the states in which they are located. As defined by the NIGC, Class I gaming—those purely social games or offering only small prizes—remain under the sole jurisdiction of the tribe. Class II bingo and other games—like poker, in which only the players' money is at stake—still fell under tribal governance but also became subject to regulation by the NIGC. All other gambling—slot machines, casino games, horse and dog racing, etc., is defined as Class III. For a tribe to build a casino (Class III), it must work with the NIGC to negotiate with the states in which its land is located. These compacts set the percentages of resulting revenues states will garner from Indian casino/resorts. Today, many states are pushing for more, in defiance of NIGC regulations.

The Bureau of Indian Affairs reported in 1999 that 212 tribes in 24 states operated 267 casinos. The numbers have grown since that time, although there continues to be dissension in Indian Country over casino operations. Some Indian nations are reluctant to undertake the expense necessary for casino construction because they are too isolated to bring in the tourists necessary to make gaming a success. Others fear the intrusion of so many non-Indian peoples in their midst. Almost all are torn by the debate between those (primarily traditionalists) who oppose gambling and others who see it as the only alternative for tribal economic viability in the twenty-first century. Often all of these motives are in play. But the bottom line is that economic self-sufficiency is necessary to maintain tribal sovereignty. With that goal in mind, many Indian nations and bands are exploring gaming as a tribal industry.

Where casino gambling has proven to be a success, the windfall of profits has benefited Indian peoples and their non-Indian neighbors as well. First and foremost, gaming produces so many jobs that on some reservations, the number of non-Indian employees is greater than the number of Indian peoples working in the casino/resort operations. In other cases, tribes have voluntarily contributed money to the state. In California, for example, the San Manuel Band of Mission Indians gave $4 million to the UCLA Law School to establish a new center of Indian Studies.[98] They donated an additional $1 million to disaster relief after the area was stripped by wildfires in 2003.

Nonetheless, states are continuing to oppose this effort to create tribal self-sufficiency by either blocking casino gambling outright or by trying to grab a greater share of the profits than is permitted to them under NIGC regulations. In some states like North Carolina, there exists a genuine dislike of all gambling, although in this case, the state has not obstructed the Eastern Band of Cherokees' gaming facilities on the Qualla Boundary in the Great Smoky Mountains. Building on the success of their first Harrah's casino, the Eastern Band of Cherokees have now undertaken construction of a second and larger casino/resort facility, using the provision of the 1982 Indian Tribal Government Tax Status Act that permits them to issue tax-exempt revenue bonds.[99] But all of these operations will be on reservation land. In Louisiana, on the other hand, when the Jena Band of Choctaws proposed to build a casino in the town of Logansport, the state legislature refused to enter compact negotiations, claiming that the citizens of Louisiana did not want gambling in their midst.[100]

Reinvesting Money Obtained through Gaming Operations

Indian tribes will not be able to protect political sovereignty unless they can create reservation economies that will provide them with the means to take care of their own people. Various strategies have been employed to draw businesses onto the reservations, to use tourism to gain revenue, to create Indian-owned operations, and perhaps most successfully to engage in gaming/resort operations. In the 1980s, this largely meant establishing bingo parlors. The revenues gained through bingo quickly drew state attention and began the struggle that continues today, as the states try to challenge Indian sovereignty in order to profit from Indian gaming. Donald L. Fixico, a Creek-Seminole-Shawnee-Sac and Fox historian offers his observations of what his people have done in Oklahoma to put the monies gained from bingo into programs to improve life for the tribe as a whole:

> They're not just taking the money and expanding into other bingo complexes. They're taking the bingo money and, for example in the Creek Nation, putting it into their own hospital; . . . they have a staff with Indian nurses and Indian doctors. They're taking that money and putting it into scholarship money for college aid . . . They've reinvested that money back into the tribe, into various . . . social services to help their own people: a tribal elderly program, a feeding program, a nursing program, and all kinds of things like that, in addition to putting much of the money into a kind of war chest . . . the Bingo operations of the tribes of Oklahoma have banded together into a coalition and the state government attorneys are restudying tribal sovereignty to tax bingo tribes. It's going to be a war of economics.*

* Peter Nabokov, *Native American Testimony* (New York: Penguin Putnam, Inc., 1991), 424–425.

Some state governments oppose federal recognition for tribes living within their borders, and other states try to block tribes from taking land already on the reservation into trust in fear that the tribe's only goal is to build a casino. Lower Brule Sioux Tribal Chairman Michael Jandreau argues that "fear of gaming is just that: a fear." Tribes have other reasons for seeking federal recognition and gaining land so that their citizens may have tax-free property for home construction and tribal economic development projects.[101]

In other cases, state opposition to Indian casino gambling has no moral basis. Rather, it is simply a question of denying profits to Indian people and grabbing those funds for the state. One of the most flagrant examples of this type of activity occurred in Maine in November 2003, when the state voted down a $650 million casino project proposed by the Penobscots and Passamaquoddies so that they could create jobs for their young people. That same day, Maine voters approved a plan to add slot machines at the state's harness racing tracks.

In Wisconsin, Governor Jim Doyle, a Democrat, signed contracts with the tribes to permit gambling, but the Republican-controlled legislature has filed suit, petitioning the courts to void these Indian gaming agreements.[102] The states' ability to play hardball is more clear in Minnesota, where a fifteen-year-old agreement between the tribes and the state leading to the operation of eighteen tribal casinos is under attack by Governor Tim Pawlenty, who may bring in state-sanctioned competition, that is, negotiate with casino businesses to open operations off the reservation, unless the tribes renegotiate their existing agreement to the state's advantage.[103] In October 2004, Pawlenty made the threat clear. He demanded the tribes pay the state $350 million annually. At the same time, his chief of staff reported that the state was negotiating with three of the largest casino developers in the country—Harrah's, MGM Grand, and Mandalay Bay—as a back-up plan if the tribes refuse to pay. "He's trying to use this [demand for $350 million]

In March 2004, casino workers protested outside the state capitol in St. Paul, Minnesota, after Governor Tim Pawlenty demanded that the state's casino tribes share $350 million of their revenues with the state. The "tax" on the state's tribes is 155 percent higher than the average tax levied on corporations.

as a de facto tax on the tribes," says Helen Blue-Redner, chairwoman of the Upper Sioux Community. "This is not allowed within the bounds of the Indian Gaming Regulatory Act of 1988, and he knows it."[104]

Other states are following Minnesota's lead. California, Florida, and Washington voters have all found referendum issues on recent ballots calling for expansion of non-tribal gambling, ostensibly to provide tax relief—always a popular incentive. But the real goal is to force Indian tribes already engaged in gaming to pay the state's ill-disguised extortion. These states have given the tribes an ultimatum: Either agree to turn over percentages of profits in excess of those permitted by the National Indian Gaming Commission or the states will bring in developers to draw business away from the Indian casinos.

State greed in trying to find ways to siphon away monies

gained by reservation casinos and resorts is best viewed as part of a continuing pattern in American history. Indian peoples have faced the theft of their land and resources since the time of first European contact. Over the last five hundred years, Indian peoples have been divested of the majority of what they owned. In the beginning, Europeans came for land—the Spanish seeking gold, the French finding wealth in the beaver trade, and the English steadily expanding away from the Atlantic Seaboard and onto lands that had been home to Indian peoples for thousand of years. Any news of Indian riches only speeded up that process of divestiture. When gold was discovered at Dahlonega, the State of Georgia, supported by President Andrew Jackson, pressed for Cherokee Removal. It was rumors of gold in the Black Hills that led Custer to make his infamous 1874 expedition into the heart of Lakota holy lands, a final straw provoking the Great Sioux War of 1875–1877. When Oklahomans discovered that Indian peoples had been settled on land containing a new kind of gold (oil) in the early twentieth century, the state began a process of declaring Indian owners incompetent, making them wards of the state so their assets could be taken from them.[105] Under the General Allotment Act, two-thirds of all reservation lands were taken away from Indian peoples between 1887 and 1934. United States Termination Policy, beginning with the formation of the Indian Claims Commission in 1946, further displaced Indian peoples and destroyed successful businesses Indian peoples had developed, such as the Menominee lumber industries in Wisconsin.

The current state efforts to violate federal law as laid out in the Indian Gaming Regulatory Act are just one more chapter in a long history of greed and theft. In 2004, the *Washington Post* uncovered evidence of a particularly naked scheme to steal money from Indian tribes. Two years earlier, a Washington, D.C., lobbyist and a public relations consultant working with conservative religious activist Ralph Reed helped the State of

Texas close the Tigua tribe's casino. Almost immediately, these two men then persuaded the tribe to pay $4.2 million to win their support in persuading Congress to reopen the Speaking Rock Casino in El Paso. They further solicited $300,000 in political contributions from the tribe, promising support from the Senate and House of Representatives. Fortunately, *Washington Post* reporters secured e-mails confirming these allegations, as well as these men's political ties to House Majority Leader Tom Delay (R-Texas). The matter is now under FBI and Senate Indian Affairs Committee investigation.[106]

Less overt but still suspicious activity has marred California's relationship with its Indian peoples. Governor Arnold Schwarzenegger refuses contributions from Indian tribes that own casinos, while his government attempts to renegotiate their compacts with the state, which were first coordinated by the NIGC. But at the same time, one of his top consultants, Mike Murphy, accepted a six-figure commission to undertake an advertising campaign on behalf of five California Indian tribes that operate casinos. At the least, this sort of activity raises questions of conflict of interest.[107]

In New York, Governor Pataki has become an active proponent of Indian casino gambling. He certainly does not support Indian peoples, which has been demonstrated by his stand on the issues of reservation tobacco and gas shops. He is, however, concerned about Indian land claims. In 1985, the Oneida Nation won an important battle when the courts ruled that Indian property brought under the Trade and Intercourse Act were still in effect, which opened the door for the Oneidas to claim lands lost to them. Most of that property is now in the hands of non-Indian peoples who bought it in good faith and understandably are upset at the idea that they are being held accountable for mistakes in policy made by people long dead.[108] At present, Governor Pataki is negotiating with five New York Indian nations, offering a settlement that would

enable the tribes to build five casinos within ninety miles of
Manhattan over the next several years in return for their forfei-
ture of their claims to hundreds of thousands of acres in the
Catskill Mountains.[109]

States' Rights to Natural Resources on Indian Land

Although casino gambling seems to be at the forefront of most
news affecting Indian nations and the states in which they are
located, it is not the only issue pitting the tribes against the
states and nearby non-Indian communities. In the West, the
states, local municipalities, and Indian tribal governments continue to tussle over scarce water resources. In the 1970s through
the 1990s, the Native American Rights Fund provided its legal
expertise to many Western Indians and was successful in protecting Indian rights to water for their fishing hatcheries and
for irrigation of farmlands. But the growing hostility of the
courts over the last couple of decades has convinced NARF
attorneys that they can better serve Indian peoples by promoting legislation and assisting in compact resolution. In Arizona,
NARF helped negotiate the Fort McDowell Indian Community
Water Rights Settlement Act and provided similar assistance to
the Northern Cheyenne tribe in reaching an agreement with
Montana to reserve water for the tribe.[110]

    NARF has also helped several tribes resist state attempts to
impose taxes. This issue of state authority is central to the concept of Indian sovereignty. If the states are allowed to impose
their will on reservation communities and businesses, the
livelihoods of many Indian citizens will be lost. Worse, tribal
governments depend on those revenues. If the state can tax
Indian residents on the reservation or anywhere in Indian
Country (including Oklahoma, where formal reservations are
not recognized), then nearly two hundred years of federal
Indian policy based on the Marshall decision of "domestic
dependent nations" would come to an end.

    Indian peoples do not seek confrontation, they prefer

instead to reach settlements with their non-Indian neighbors that will allow all to benefit from sharing either natural resources, such as water in the West, or through revenues produced by successful business ventures, such as those earned by the Mississippi Band of Choctaw. The last two decades have demonstrated that when Indian peoples prosper, they improve the community around them by providing jobs, contributing monies to educational and other local services, etc. The states have always been greedy for more. But Indian peoples must protect their rights to self-rule and self-determination. To that end, the work goes forward as tribes continue to petition for federal recognition, as they resist state inroads on their self-government, and as they seek to regain land or negotiate settlements for what was stolen. Most importantly, Indian nations are trying to find ways to live in peace with the states and their neighboring communities, while maintaining their sovereign right to exist as nations within a nation.[111]

8

Sovereignty and
Self-Determination

Considerable archaeological evidence as well as the oral histories of Indian peoples exists to prove that Indians employed a wide variety of means of self-governance for thousands of years before European contact. In some regions, small band organization ruled. In other areas, large societies grew with the resulting sophisticated political structures necessary for Indian peoples to evolve into nations, and in some instances, even confederacies of nations.

CAN FULL SOVEREIGNTY EXIST?

Europeans recognized the sovereignty of Indian nations and guaranteed to respect them in numerous treaties. Beginning with the Constitution (Article I, Section 8) and the Northwest Ordinance, also passed in 1787, the United States similarly recognized and pledged to honor that sovereignty. The Supreme Court provided the groundwork for modern Indian law in John Marshall's 1831 landmark decision in

President George W. Bush signs the Executive Memorandum on Tribal Sovereignty and Consultation, reaffirming the U.S. government's legal and political relationship with Indian tribes. Shown here are representatives of several Indian nations who were honored during the opening ceremonies of the National Museum of the American Indian in September 2004.

Cherokee Nation v. Georgia, citing Indian peoples as "domestic dependent nations." Proof that the U.S. government viewed Indian peoples as distinct nations can be found in the four hundred treaties that it signed with various tribes prior to 1871, when Congress declared that henceforth the federal government would cease to negotiate treaties with Indian nations.

What followed was an intense attack on Indian sovereignty, as Congress pursued a policy of acculturation that included the destruction of tribal governments through the General Allotment Act, the Curtis Act, the Major Crimes Act, and other legislation designed to establish Congress' plenary power over Indian peoples. The Indian Reorganization Act in 1934 attempted to halt some of the damage that had been done and restore tribal governments. This new federal policy, which recognized cultural pluralism, that is, that no culture is superior to another and all have a right to exist, was challenged in the years following World War II, when the pendulum of federal Indian policy swung again to acculturation. Termination sought to end all treaty obligations between the U.S. government and America's Indian peoples, abrogating federal trustee obligations and reducing Indians to mere state citizens.

Restoring Tribal Government Authority

The passage of the 1975 Indian Self-Determination and Education Assistance Act went a long way to restoring tribal government authority. Since 1975, Indian nations, bands, and communities have been able to oversee operation of federal programs in health care, education, and other services on their reservations. After so many centuries of assault on their communities, it is little wonder that considerable dissension exists among many tribes, as competing factions vie for political control. But this is the nature of politics in every culture: the electoral process is marked more by conflict than consensus.

Internal political factionalism among Indian tribes is abetted by the dual citizenship of Indian peoples. As citizens of the United States as well as their individual nations, Indians have access to the federal courts, as well as the Bureau of Indian Affairs (BIA) within the Department of the Interior. Both the Department of the Interior, as well as the federal courts, has been swamped with suits brought before them as Indian people compete for political control.

Significant issues exist today to divide Indian peoples, the most notorious and colorful example being casino gambling. Many fear that casinos will bring unwanted intrusions onto the reservation. Others oppose it as being contrary to traditional cultural values. In 2004, Vernon Masayesva urged his fellow Hopis to vote no to a proposed casino construction project near Winslow, Arizona, because he believes the Hopis must honor their ancestors who had created a sanctuary in the desert country in order that they might follow *Haso'gada's* way of life. "They were refugees running away to escape Koyaanisqatsi, a world turned upside down. Here on the fingerprints of Black Mesa, they found the place." Tribal Vice Chairman Caleb Johnson explains the matter more directly: "Gaming is making money off other people's bad habits, and the Hopi way says we should not use other people's bad habits to benefit."[112]

Other Indian tribes see casino gambling as the only alternative to achieving economic viability—a vital component to ensuring tribal self-sufficiency and therefore Indian self-determination. To that end, many Indian nations, even those who long opposed gambling, such as the Senecas and, most recently, one chapter house of the Navajos, have undertaken casino/resort operations, sparking still more dissension among the people of these nations.

The Need for Unity

Many worry about the factionalism that exists within many tribes. Competition has always been present, as evidenced by clans, which were based on well-established kinship systems that ruled in the past. Warrior societies came into being on the Great Plains, at least in part to enforce compliance among the bands of the nation when unity was necessary— for the autumn buffalo hunt or for defense in times of war. In modern-day America, the need for unity among Indian peoples is greater than ever. And if there are issues that divide Indian nations, there are even more that exist to bring them together.

Today, the struggle continues as Indian tribes must face considerable opposition from corporate and state interests that seek to divest Indians of their lands and resources. Organizations like the Native American Rights Fund provide lawyers, many of whom are enrolled members of Indian nations, to help litigate and, when possible, negotiate agreements to protect the interests and welfare of Indian peoples.[113]

Full sovereignty may no longer exist. Tribal governments retain full control over some issues such as enrollment, and they have the authority to determine who can be enrolled as a member of the nation and who cannot, a right that has been upheld by the federal courts from *Elk v. Wilkins* (1884) through *Santa Clara v. Martinez* (1978). In other areas, they must share authority. Federal courts may overrule tribal courts. Tribal police have sole jurisdiction over some crimes committed on the reservation, but not the majority of felonies as outlined in the Major Crimes Act of 1885. Many nations have worked out cross-deputation agreements with surrounding counties that permit cooperation between law enforcement officers on and off the reservation.

The 1975 Indian Self-Determination and Education Assistance Act, as well as some of the other legislation of the 1970s discussed previously, restored considerable authority to tribal governments. Today, tribes may enter compacts with the U.S. Department of the Interior to manage BIA health, education, and other services on the reservation. They now have the authority to protect their children from being taken away to be raised in non-Indian families. Still, Congress retains plenary power and a self-defined trustee responsibility to Indian peoples. Treaty obligations continue to exist. Indian peoples ceded so much over the last two hundred years of American history in return for promises of federal protection. Those safeguards are vital today to protect tribes from the states and corporate interests that would ignore tribal authority, as well as federal laws. The question remains: Will the federal court uphold the law and treaty obligations or will the Supreme Court abrogate its responsibilities, returning case after case to the state courts, essentially instituting Termination yet again?

Urban Indians

The question of political issues among Indian peoples does not end at the reservation borders. Today, more Native Americans live off the reservation than on the reservation, although the 2000 U.S. Census for the first time revealed a reversal in numbers. Some Indians are now returning to the reservation, a move made possible, no doubt, by the job opportunities now available through tribal efforts to create successful business enterprises on the reservation.[114] But the fact remains that the majority of Indian peoples live apart from their tribes in communities across the United States.

Sometimes referred to as "urban Indians," these people find their political voice through a plethora of Pan-Indian organizations. Indian centers exist in every major city, providing a place where people may come together. They may not share a tribal identity, but they can celebrate their common Indianness. Publications such as *Indian Country Today* provide the latest news on issues facing the nations. Tribal Web sites also exist to promote awareness among those who live far from the reservation. At every election, the Cherokee Nation's Web site includes long editorials on which candidates are friendly to Indian issues and which are not. The Seneca Nation's Web site devotes considerable space to their "Honor Indian Treaties" campaign, part of their ongoing battle to protect reservation businesses from state attempts to collect taxes to which they have no right. On the national level, the interests of all Indian peoples continues to be brought forward by the National Congress of American Indians.[115]

For urban Indians, their reservation homelands continue to be vitally important as places where they may return and bring their children so that the next generation may learn to value their identity as Indians, albeit as Indians of many different tribes—the result of mixed marriages common among Indians living away from the reservation. Still, the homeland serves as a place of renewal, where heritage may be celebrated.

As Janet McCloud, the late Tulalip Reservation activist once put it: "When all is going crazy . . . our people can come back to the center to find the calming effect; to reconnect with their spiritual self."[116] Mary Thomas, lieutenant governor of the Gila

Learning To Be American Indian

One of the principal challenges facing Indian peoples is keeping culture alive for future generations. Today, the majority of Indians live away from the reservation. Their children may be the product of mixed-marriage and are, in any case, growing up in cities far removed from their homeland. Thus, the task of imbuing that sense of who they are as Indians becomes harder. Yet, one Ojibwa parent finds hope in seeing that new generations are seeking identity by returning to the tribes of their grandparents. The passage that follows emphasizes how important the survival of the reservations and the political sovereignty necessary to protect those lands is for those young people trying to find their roots. Indian tribal governments and the homelands they safeguard must continue to exist not only for the sake of today's children but for the generations to come. All have a right to be proud of their Indian identity.

> Now my children are urging me to recall all the stories and bits of information that I ever heard my grandparents or any of the older Ojibway tell. It is important, they say, because now their children are asking them. Others are saying the same thing. It is well that they are asking, for the Ojibway young must learn their cycle. . . . The children of our people who come to our agency have a questioning look, a dubious but seeking-to-learn look, and I truly believe that they are reaching back to learn those things of which they can be proud. Many of these children were born and raised in the urban areas and they do not make any distinctions as to their tribes. They do not say, "I am Ojibway," or "I am Dakota," or "I am Arapaho," but they say, "I am an Indian." Now they, too, are looking to their tribal identity.*

*   Ignatia Broker, *Night Flying Woman: An Ojibway Narrative* (St. Paul, Minn.: Minnesota Historical Society Press, 1983), 1–7, in Colin Calloway, *First Peoples: A Documentary Survey of American Indian History* (Boston, Mass.: Bedford/St. Martin's Press, 2004), 443–445.

River Community, refers to the reservation as "this land that we hold so precious to our hearts."[117]

Determining Their Own Fate

Protection of the homeland for the welfare of all Indian peoples remains the primary responsibility of tribal governments. In order for the reservations to continue to exist as viable economic and social communities, the tribal governments designated by Indian peoples must be in place. No individual or political group ever possesses complete sovereignty or self-determination. All are impacted by events from outside. This is true of every government that has existed in history. It also applies to Indian peoples.

However, sovereignty does continue to exist. Indian peoples simply refuse to cede it. Indians have always been the chief determinants of their own fate. That they have survived against overwhelming forces brought against them during the course of the last five hundred years should serve as proof that Indian peoples are here to stay. The Indian nations, their sovereignty recognized and guaranteed by U.S. law and even more by their own people, will continue to function under political systems of their own choosing. The battle to protect their cultural integrity and their right to exist as separate entities, that is, nations within a nation, will not be easy. But it never has been.

Among many Indian peoples there remains a basic acknowledgment of an ancient seven/seven rule. That is, they must protect what seven generations past left to them. It is a debt they owe to honor those ancestors. Equally important, they are the current trustees of the responsibility to protect their lands and their cultural identities for seven generations yet to come. Indian nations will find a way to work through the myriad of complex political issues facing them today to fulfill that trust.

c. 5000 B.C.	Extension of agriculture and onset of permanent Indian settlements.
A.D. 700	First appearance of mound builder culture in lower Mississippi Valley.
900–1300s	Anasazi culture flourishes in the Southwest.
Late 1400s	Formation of the Iroquois (Haudenosaunee) Confederacy.
1754	Onset of French and Indian War.
1755	Atkin Report outlining the power of Indian nations.
1761	Pontiac's Pan-Indian Confederacy movement.
1784	Treaty of Fort Stanwix: peace agreement between the United States and the Iroquois.
1785	Treaty of Hopewell: the first treaty signed between the Cherokee Nation and the United States.
1787	U.S. Constitution acknowledges sovereignty of Indian tribes; Northwest Ordinance adopted by Congress guaranteeing federal recognition of tribal sovereignty.
1824	Bureau of Indian Affairs established.
1830	Congress passes the Indian Removal Act.
1831	*Cherokee Nation v. Georgia*: Indian Tribes are "domestic dependent nations."
1846	*United States v. Rogers*: Supreme Court defines who is Indian.
1849	Bureau of Indian Affairs transferred from the War Department to the Department of the Interior.
1869–71	Ely Parker (Seneca) serves as the first Indian Commissioner of Indian Affairs.
1871	End of treaty negotiations with Indian tribes.
1882	Organization of Indian Rights Association.
1884	*Elk v. Wilkins*: Supreme Court restores tribal authority to determine membership.
1885	Seven Major Crimes Act.
1886	*Eastern Band of Cherokee v. U.S. and Cherokee Nation West.*
1887	Congress passes the General Allotment Act.
1890	Indian Naturalization Act.

1898   Curtis Act terminates governments in Indian Territory; Assimilative Crime Act passed by Congress.

1911   Organization of the Society of American Indians.

1924   Indian Citizenship Act.

1926   Organization of the National Council of American Indians.

1934   Congress passes the Indian Reorganization Act.

1944   Organization of the National Congress of American Indians.

1946   Indian Claims Commission created to end treaty commitments and eliminate tribal governments.

1953   Congress passes Termination Resolution and Public Law 280.

1961   National Indian Youth Council established.

1963   *Arizona v. California.*

1968   American Indian Movement organizes.

1970   Peter MacDonald first elected chairman of Navajo Nation; Native American Rights Fund established.

1972   Indian Education Act.

1974   Indian Financing Act.

1975   Indian Self-Determination and Education Assistance Act passed; Council of Energy Resource Tribes (CERT) is formed; restoration of the Menominee Indian Reservation.

1978   *Santa Clara v. Martinez*; Indian Religious Freedom and Indian Civil Rights Act; Indian Child Welfare Act; *United States v. Wheeler*; *Oliphant v. Suquamish Indian Tribe.*

1979   Phillip Martin elected chairman of the Mississippi Band of Choctaw.

1980   Maine Indian Claims Settlement Act.

1981   *Montana v. United States.*

1982   Indian Tribal Government Tax Status Act passed by Congress.

1988   Indian Gaming Regulatory Act passed by Congress.

1997   New York State Police surround the Seneca Cattaraugus Reservation.

2004   National Museum of the American Indian opens in Washington, D.C.

Notes

Chapter 1:
Early Political Development

1 Colin Calloway, *First Peoples: A Documentary Survey of American Indian History* (Boston, Mass.: Bedford/St. Martin's Press, 2004), 22.

2 Arrell Gibson, *The American Indian: Prehistory to the Present* (Lexington, Mass.: D.C. Heath and Company, 1980), 43.

3 Deborah Welch, *Virginia: An Illustrated History* (New York: Hippocrene Books, 2005), 19.

4 Virginius Dabney, *Virginia: The New Dominion* (New York: Doubleday and Company, Inc., 1956), 11.

5 Submitted by Edmond Atkin, a member of the South Carolina colonial council, found in Gibson, *The American Indian: Prehistory to the Present*, 232.

6 Francis Paul Prucha, ed. *Documents of United States Indian Policy* (Lincoln, Nebr.: University of Nebraska Press, 1975), 10.

Chapter 2:
Domestic Dependent Nations

7 See Arthur C. Parker, *The Code of Handsome Lake* (Albany, N.Y., New York State Museum, 1911, reprinted in 1990).

8 R. David Edmunds, "American History, Tecumseh, and the Shawnee Prophet," *Major Problems in American Indian History*, Albert L. Hurtado and Peter Iverson, eds. (Lexington, Mass.: D.C. Heath and Company, 1994), 197.

9 H.B. Cushman, *History of the Choctaw, Chickasaw and Natchez Indians* (Greenville, Tex.: 1899), 310, in Steven Mintz, ed., *Native American Voices: A History and Anthology* (St. James, N.Y.: Brandywine Press, 1995), 99.

10 Gibson, 325.

11 *Cherokee Nation v. Georgia*, 1831.

12 Calloway, 276.

13 Peter Iverson, *The Navajos* (New York: Chelsea House Publishers, 1990), 46.

14 John Collier, *The Indians of the Americas* (New York: W.W. Norton and Company, 1947), 15–16.

15 Lawrence C. Kelly, "The Indian Reorganization Act: The Dream and the Reality," *The American Indian Past and Present*, Roger L. Nichols, ed. (New York: Alfred A. Knopf, 1986), 244.

16 Paul L. Hallam to Joe Jennings, Field Administrator Indian Organization, November 13, 1935, Yankton Box 3, University of South Dakota Archives.

17 For more about John Collier and the failure of the Indian Reorganization Act, see Kenneth Philip, *John Collier's Crusade for Indian Reform, 1920–1954* (Tucson, Ariz.: University of Arizona Press, 1977) and Lawrence C. Kelly, *The Assault on Assimilationism: John Collier and the Origins of Indian Policy Reform* (Albuquerque, N.M.: University of New Mexico Press, 1983).

18 For a quick overview of Ira Hayes' service, please visit the following Website: *www.arlingtoncemetery.net/irahayes.htm.*

Chapter 3:
Pan-Indianism

19 D'Arcy McNickle, *Native American Tribalism: Indian Survivals and Renewals* (New York: Oxford University Press, 1973), 82.

20 "Statement of Goals," Second annual conference of the Society of American Indians, 1912, *Arthur C. Parker Papers*, New York State Museum, Albany, N.Y.

21 The 1900 U.S. Census recorded approximately 250,000 Indians remaining in the United States, all that were left of the millions who had once lived in this country.

22 For an excellent biography of this remarkable man, see Peter Iverson, *Carlos Montezuma and the Changing World of American Indians*, 2nd edition (Albuquerque, N.M.: University of New Mexico Press, 2001).

23 Laura Cornelius Kellogg, "Some Facts and Figures on Indian Education," *Quarterly Journal* 2 (April–June 1913): 36–46.

24 Carlos Montezuma, "Let My People Go," presented at the Society of American Indians' annual conference in 1915, *Papers of the Indian Rights Association* (Philadelphia, Pa.).

25 *American Indian Life*, Bulletin No. 5 (April–June 1926), *Papers of the Indian Rights Association.*

26 G.E. Lindquist, *A Handbook for Missionary Workers among the American Indians* (1928), *Papers of the Indian Rights Association.*

27 "Petition of the National Council of American Indians," *Congressional Record* (April 24, 1926)

discussed in Jennings C. Wise, *The Red Man in the New World Drama: A Politico-Legal Study with a Pageantry of American Indian History* (Washington, D.C.: W.F. Roberts Co., 1931).

28 Ibid., 574.

29 John Collier to Raymond and Gertrude Bonnin, March 4, 1932, *Papers of John Collier*, (Yale University).

30 Statement of Purpose in the *American Indian Magazine* (Oklahoma, 1927).

31 The best discussion of fraternal Pan-Indianism, as well as early reform political Pan-Indian societies, can be found in Hazel W. Hertzberg, *The Search for an American Indian Identity: Modern Pan-Indian Movements* (Syracuse, N.Y.: Syracuse University Press, 1971).

32 Peter Nabokov, *Native American Testimony* (New York: Penguin Putnam, Inc, 1999), 356.

Chapter 4:
Tribal Membership and Governance

33 *Elk v. Wilkins* (1884).

34 United States Census, April 1, 2004. See the Census Bureau's website at *www.census.gov*.

35 *United States v. Rogers*, 1846.

36 *Eastern Band of Cherokee Indians v. U.S. and Cherokee Nation, West*, 1886.

37 *Santa Clara v. Martinez*, 1978.

38 For a current study of how mixed-blood Utes continue to seek their right to tribal membership, see R. Warren Metcalf, *Termination's Legacy: The Discarded Indians of Utah* (Lincoln, Nebr.: University of Nebraska Press, 2002).

39 "Query: CDIB Card and Tribal Membership," *H-AmIndian* (Part of the H-Net resources and housed with the Department of History, Arizona State University), February 22, 2005.

40 Jacob Jordan, "Two American Indian Tribes Receive State Recognition," Associated Press, February 17, 2005.

41 Joane Nagel, *American Indian Ethnic Renewal: Red Power and the Resurgence of Identity and Culture* (New York: Oxford University Press, 1996), 202–203.

42 Donald L. Fixico, *Urban Indians* (New York: Chelsea House Publishers, 1981), 95. For a more in-depth treatment of the subject, see Fixico, *The Urban Indian Experience in*

America (Albuquerque, N.M.: University of New Mexico Press, 2000).

43 Brad Agnew, "Wilma Mankiller," *The New Warriors: Native American Leaders since 1900*, R. David Edmunds, ed. (Nebraska, Nebr.: University of Nebraska Press, 2001), 223.

44 See the Seneca Nation's website at *www.sni.org*.

45 Sidney L. Harring, "Indian Law, Sovereignty, and State Law," *A Companion to American Indian History*, Philip J. Deloria and Neal Salisbury, eds. (Malden, Mass.: Blackwell Publishers, Inc., 2002), 446–447.

46 Vine Deloria, Jr. and Clifford M. Lytle, *American Indians, American Justice* (Austin, Tex.: University of Texas Press, 1983), 112.

47 Ibid., 108–109.

48 Calloway, 468.

49 For a listing of laws applying to American Indian peoples including a short synopsis of each, please see William N. Thompson, *Native American Issues: A Reference Handbook* (Santa Barbara: ABC-CLIO, Inc., 1996).

Chapter 5:
Tribal Factionalism

50 Loretta Fowler, *Tribal Sovereignty and the Historical Imagination: Cheyenne-Arapaho Politics* (Lincoln, Nebr.: University of Nebraska Press, 2002).

51 Frederic J. Frommer, "Group Says Indians Suffer from Substandard Housing," Associated Press, September 20, 2004.

52 For a readily accessible account of Martin's contributions, see Benton R. White and Christine Schultz White, "Phillip Martin: Mississippi Choctaw," *The New Warriors: Native American Leaders since 1900*, R. David Edmunds, ed. (Lincoln, Nebr.: University of Nebraska Press, 2001), 195–210.

53 Debbie Elliott, "Mississippi Choctaws Find Economic Success," National Public Radio broadcast. (July 17, 2004). For full interview of *All Things Considered* segment, access the audio option on the following web page: *www.npr.org/features*. Interested readers may also wish to visit the Choctaw Website at *www.choctaw.org*.

54 John Finger writes of how tales of Dragging Canoe's exploits inspired later generations in

his book, *The Eastern Band of Cherokees, 1819–1900* (Knoxville, Tenn.: University of Tennessee Press, 1984), 84.

55 Calloway, 175–176.

56 Donald L. Fixico, "Tribal Leaders and the Demand for Natural Energy Resources on Reservation Lands," *The Plains Indians of the Twentieth Century,* ed. Peter Iverson (Norman, Okla.: University of Oklahoma Press, 1985), 222.

57 For the best account of Navajo politics in the twentieth century, see Peter Iverson, *The Navajo Nation* (Albuquerque, N.M.: University of New Mexico Press, 1981).

58 Calloway, 479.

59 Iverson, *The Navajos,* 99.

60 For his defense, MacDonald hired attorney, F. Lee Bailey who had already established a national reputation for representing Samuel Sheppard, the Fort Bragg doctor accused of murdering his wife—who later became the inspiration for the television series and movie, *The Fugitive.*

61 Iverson, *The Navajos,* 103.

62 Eloise Ogden, "Revising the Constitution," *Minot Daily News,* February 15, 2005.

63 Brenda Norrell, "Scientists Back Navajos Fighting Uranium Mining," *Indian Country Today,* March 12, 2004.

64 Glenn Coin, "Ganienkeh Mohawks Oppose Land Deal," *The Post-Standard,* November 25, 2004.

Chapter 6:
Federal Trustee Status

65 Abolition of Treaty Making, March 3, 1871, *U.S. Statutes at Large,* 16:566; found in Francis Paul Prucha, ed., *Documents of United States Indian Policy* (Lincoln, Nebr.: University of Nebraska Press, 1975), 136.

66 Act of March 3, 1885, 23 Statute 362, found in Sandra L. Cadwalader and Vine Deloria, Jr., eds., *The Aggressions of Civilization: Federal Indian Policy since the 1880s* (Philadelphia, Pa.: Temple University Press, 1984), 108–109.

67 Ibid., 109.

68 Gibson, 542.

69 Felix S. Cohen, *Handbook of Federal Indian Law* (Washington, D.C.: Government Printing Office, 1942), 122.

70 *United States v. Wheeler,* 1978.

71 *Oliphant v. Suquamish Indian Tribe,* 1978.

72 Cadwalader and Deloria, eds., *The Aggressions of Civilization,* 95.

73 *Duro v. Reina,* 1990.

74 Calloway, 471.

75 Sidney L. Harring, "Indian Law, Sovereignty, and State Law: Native People and the Law," *A Companion to American Indian History,* Philip J. Deloria and Neal Salisbury, eds. (Malden, Mass.: Blackwell Publishers, Inc., 2002), 443.

76 "Yakama Tribal Lockup Again Under Federal Scrutiny," The Associated Press State and Local Wire, December 30, 2004.

77 A Seneca Indian, his mother was the grand-daughter of Sosheowa, the successor of Handsome Lake. For more about Parker and his role in drawing up the terms of the Confederate surrender at Appomattox, please access *www.answers.com/topic/ely-s-parker.*

78 William T. Hagan, *American Indians* (Chicago, Ill.: University of Chicago Press, 1961), 111–112.

79 Editorial, *St. Paul Pioneer Press,* September 17, 2003.

80 Listed on H-AmIndian (February 16, 2005).

81 Calloway, 475.

82 For more information about NARF, please access the organization's web page at *www.narf.org.*

83 John R. Wunder, "Walter Echo-Hawk," *The New Warriors: Native American Leaders since 1900* (Lincoln, Nebr.: University of Nebraska Press, 201), 305.

84 See "Comments by U.S. Senate Candidate Tom Coburn (August 21, 2004) and "Yes on SQ 712: Oklahomans for Education and Jobs," on the Nation's Website: *www.cherokee.org.*

85 James W. Brosnan, "Both Sides Coveting the Indian Electorate," *Albuquerque Tribune,* September 24, 2004.

Chapter 7:
Sovereignty versus the States

86 Glenn Coin, "Indians Owe Taxes, Most in Poll Say," *The Post-Standard,* January 6, 2005.

87 "Mississippi Choctaws Provide Economic Boost to State According to Mississippi State University Study," Mississippi Band of Choctaw Indians Press Room (December 6, 2001). For full article, see

www.choctaw.org/press_room/2001Archive/pr_2001_12_06.html.

88 *Cherokee Nation v. Georgia*, 1831.

89 Patricia K. Ourada, *The Menominee* (New York: Chelsea House Publishers, 1990), 95–101

90 John R. Wunder, "Walter Echo-Hawk," *The New Warriors: Native American Leaders since 1900*, R. David Edmunds, ed. (Lincoln, Nebr.: University of Nebraska Press, 2001), 305.

91 Welch, *Virginia: An Illustrated History*, 24.

92 Hope Yen, "High Court to Review Indian Reservation Fuel Tax," Associated Press, February 28, 2005, found on H-AmIndian site.

93 This author was among those trapped on the Cattaraugus Reservation and witnessed the events of April 1997.

94 For more information about the Honor Indian Treaties campaign, please access the Website of the Seneca Nation of Indians at *www.sni.org.*

95 My thanks to the staff at the Seneca Allegany Casino who provided information about current operations. For more information please visit their Website at *www.senecaallegany-casino.com.*

96 Calloway, 487.

97 Ibid., 486.

98 Associated Press, "Indian Tribes Funding School Projects, Endeavors," *Los Angeles Times*, April 11, 2004.

99 Kerra L. Boston, "Tribe Bets Poker Craze Will Bring Big Payoff," *Asheville* (NC) *Citizen Times* (January 12, 2005). For more information about Harrah's casino operations in Cherokee, North Carolina, please access the Website: *www.harrahs.com.*

100 Chris Frink, "Foster Leaves Casino Pact on Table," *The* [Baton Rouge] *Advocate*, January 7, 2004.

101 *Tribune Business News* (Rapid City, South Dakota), *Indian Country Today*, February 16, 2005.

102 Matt Pommer, "AG Calls Bets on Casino Suit," *Capital Times*, December 8, 2003.

103 Patrick Sweeney, "Gambling Comment Tough to Interpret," *Pioneer Press*, February 6, 2004.

104 Patricia Lopez, "Pawlenty Wants Tribes to Pay $350 Million; Plan Guarantees Casino Exclusivity in Exchange for Annual Payment," *Minneapolis Star Tribune*, October 22, 2004.

105 An Indian Rights Association committee sent to investigate murder and corruption in Oklahoma reported findings of such atrocious cruelty that their report prompted a U.S. Senate investigation. See *Oklahoma's Poor Rich Indians* (Philadelphia, Pa.: Indian Rights Association, 1924).

106 Susan Schmidt, "Insiders Worked Both Sides of Gaming Issue," *Washington Post*, September 26, 2004.

107 Dan Morain, "Interest Groups Retain Advisor to Governor," *Los Angeles Times*, September 27, 2004.

108 Calloway, 470.

109 Brian McGuire, "Indians Backing Pataki's Land Pact," *New York Sun*, March 1, 2005.

110 Wunder, 307.

111 For a list of cases currently being assisted by the Native American Rights Fund, please access the NARF Website at *www.narf.org/cases/index.html.*

Chapter 8:
Sovereignty and Self-Determination

112 Brenda Norrell, "Hopi Voters Reject Gaming: Votes Lean toward Traditional Path," *Indian Country Today*, May 28, 2004.

113 For information on the background of NARF attorneys and the cases with which they have worked, please consult the NARF web page at *www.narf.org.*

114 United States Census, April 1, 2004, accessible through Website at *www.factfinder.census.gov.* For more information, see the U.S. Census Bureau's Website at *www.census.gov/population/www/socdemo/race/indian/html.*

115 For more information about the NCAI, please visit their Website at *www.ncai.org.* News of the Cherokee Nation may be found at *www.cherokee.org.* The Seneca Nation's Website is *www.sni.org.*

116 Mark N. Trahant, "The Center of Everything," *Seattle Times*, June 4, 1999.

117 Brenda Norrell, "American Indians' Convention in Arizona Focuses on Booming Construction Sector," *Indian Country Today*, May 19, 2004.

Glossary

Allotment—Individual land holdings used as part of federal policy to encourage settlement of the trans-Mississippi West through the Homestead Acts of 1862 and 1864 that provided 160 acres for a nominal fee to anyone willing to live on and improve the property. Later, Congress used the principle of allotment to divide Indian reservations through the General Allotment Act (sometimes called the Dawes Severalty Act) in 1887.

Americanization Policy—The guiding principle of various U.S. Indian policies throughout the nineteenth and twentieth centuries, Americanization sought to destroy Indian cultures and transform the people into white middle-class farmers and ranchers. Key to this policy was the destruction of tribal governments as central to the promotion of acculturation.

assimilation—The process of trying to absorb a minority group within the political, social, and economic folds of the majority society—in this case, the term was sometimes adopted as a policy goal by the federal government determined to destroy Indian nations and transform their people into Anglo-Americans.

Bureau of Indian Affairs—The BIA functions as the agency within the Department of Interior responsible for Indian affairs. Originally designed to manage relations between the federal government and the tribes, the BIA served throughout most of the twentieth century as a sort of "Big Brother," overseeing first the destruction of tribal governments, and after 1934, shaping new tribal constitutions, economic development, and other social programs. Now Indian nations have assumed responsibility for their own political and economic development, relegating the BIA to an advisory capacity, still responsible for promoting educational, health, and economic programs. The BIA determines which tribes will be recognized by the federal government and which people (regardless of tribal enrollment) will be identified as Indian.

cultural pluralism—Recognition that other societies and cultures may be different from one's own but they possess equal value—they have the right to exist.

Curtis Act—Passed by Congress on June 28, 1898, this law abolished the tribal courts of governments of the Five Civilized Tribes in Indian Territory—the Cherokee, Chickasaw, Choctaw, Creek, and Seminole nations.

enrollment—A term that refers to an individual's membership within a specific Indian tribe, band, or community. Longstanding U.S. policy has left it to the Indian nations to determine who qualified for inclusion on their tribal rolls.

General Allotment Act—Also known as the Dawes Severalty Act, this Congressional legislation was designed to break up Indian reservations, destroying traditional communal lifestyles and economies, thereby forcing acculturation by encouraging Indian peoples to embrace the concept of private property. Passed in 1887, the law took approximately two-thirds of reservation land away from Indian peoples and sold it to non-Indians. The proceeds of these sales were ostensibly to be used for Indian welfare but the money disappeared.

House Concurrent Resolution 108 (Termination Resolution)—This 1953 federal law outlined the steps to be taken to terminate all economic support and services guaranteed to Indian tribes by past treaties. All Indian nations in New York, California, Florida, and Texas were to be terminated immediately along with other tribes, specifically targeted because of the rich resources on their lands.

Indian Child Welfare Act—In 1978, Congress put an end to the practice of placing Indian children in adoptive homes away from the reservation. Under this act, children who lose their parents are entrusted to the custody of their extended family. In the event that family is unavailable, the tribe will oversee adoption and foster care.

Indian Citizenship Act—This act, passed in 1924, authorized the Secretary of the Interior to issue certificates of citizenship to all Indian people born within the territorial limits of the United States.

Indian Claims Commission—Created by Congress in 1946, the ICC was charged with settling all treaty obligations with the Indian nations, thus ushering in the era of Termination. The goal was to end the federal trustee relationship between the United States and the Indian nations, rendering Indian peoples merely citizens of the states in which they resided, subject to the laws and taxes of those states; their reservations no longer accorded the federal protection guaranteed them by past treaties and the sovereignty recognized in the U.S. Constitution.

Indian Financing Act—In 1974 Congress passed this act, increasing the monies available for Indian business ventures and creating a grants program for reservation economic initiatives.

Indian Gaming Regulatory Act—Congress created the National Indian Gaming Commission in 1988 to regulate gambling on Indian lands. This law states that Indian groups may establish gambling if that form of gaming is already permitted anywhere in the state in which they reside. The act established three classes of gaming. The first, to be regulated solely by the tribe, includes traditional Indian forms of gaming for which there are only low-stake prizes. Class Two includes bingo, pull tabs, and card games that involve bets made only by the players. Class Three covers most casino activities, race betting, and lotteries and requires the tribes to enter into negotiation with the state before initiating operations.

Indian Reorganization Act—Passed by Congress in 1934, this legislation was at the heart of Commissioner of Indian Affairs, John Collier's "Indian New Deal." It contained several provisions, including an immediate end to Allotment policy; the creation of independent tribal governments; new day schools built on the reservation, where children could learn traditional culture as well as the basics of education; greater funding for tribal health care; a restoration of freedom to practice traditional religions; and monies set aside to buy back land lost under the General Allotment Act.

Indian Self-Determination and Education Assistance Act—In 1975, Congress authorized tribal governments to undertake contracts with federal agencies to administer all educational, health, and other service programs on the reservation. It also mandated that Indian parents had to be given a voice on all public school boards that accepted grants for the education of Indian children.

Major Crimes Act—Passed by Congress on March 3, 1885, the act lists seven major crimes, which, if they occurred on reservation lands, would fall under federal, rather than tribal, police jurisdiction. These crimes included murder, manslaughter, rape, assault with the intent to kill, burglary, larceny, and arson. In 1976, the act was amended to add kidnapping, incest, statutory rape, assault with the intent to commit rape, and assault with a deadly weapon.

Meriam Report—This 1928 federal study revealed the depth of Indian poverty, recommending several reforms in the areas of health care, education, and economic self-sufficiency. Its findings provided the evidence John Collier would use to push the Indian Reorganization Act through Congress in 1934.

National Congress of American Indians—This Pan-Indian group, first formed in 1944 to meet the challenges of Termination, still exists as a voice of Indian America to non-Indian America. The Congress meets annually to discuss current issues facing Indian peoples and seeks to lobby the federal government on behalf of Indian welfare.

National Indian Gaming Commission—Created by the Indian Gaming Regulatory Act of 1988, the NIGC exists to oversee gambling operations in Indian Country. Its three-member board (two of whom must be Indian) works primarily to negotiate agreements between the states and the various Indian nations. It also approves contracts between tribes and outside corporate interests willing to invest in gaming operations.

Native American Rights Fund—NARF was created in 1970 to provide legal representation and assistance to Indian tribes, organizations, and individuals throughout the United States. It acts as an advocate to protect the rights of Indian peoples, to advise on the initiation of legislation to safeguard Indian sovereignty and lands, and to educate the broader American public on Indian law, as well as current issues.

plenary power—A term that refers to the federal government's trustee oversight of Indian affairs—Indian nations, tribes, and bands are permitted to be self-governing but not truly sovereign. Congress assumes plenary control; that is, the ultimate capacity to exert its authority over Indian peoples. This principle was articulated by the Supreme

Court in *United States v. Kagama* (1886) and is sometimes called the "two-sovereignty theory."

powwow—Social gatherings that feature dancing and traditional arts and crafts, these events are now held annually on many reservations, both as a means to draw the community together and to enable non-Indians to observe ceremonies. Powwows have become an important part of the tourist industry on many reservations.

Public Law 280—Passed by Congress in 1953, this legislation gives several states jurisdiction over Indian communities, primarily in matters of land disputes. It does not give the states the power to tax sovereign Indian nations, but it opened a door through which the states can try to extend their power over Indian peoples.

Relocation Policy—Practiced by federal agents in the post-World War II decades, its goal was to encourage Indian peoples to abandon their reservation homes and travel to cities where they were promised aid in securing work and finding housing.

reservation—These were tracts of land set aside for Indian peoples. Some Indian nations, such as the Sioux, were divided among numerous reservations. In other cases, reserveations were set aside for unaffiliated Indians. Today, the reservations serve as cultural homelands and communities where Indian peoples seek economic self-sufficiency to enable them to support themselves in a lifestyle of their choosing.

sovereignty—This term refers to nationhood and self-rule. Both the Constitution and more than four hundred treaties negotiated by the U.S. government, as well as numerous state and colonial treaties, recognize the right of Indian nations to exist, to govern themselves, free of state restrictions.

Termination—Federal Indian policy practiced from the late 1940s through the 1960s to abrogate treaties and thus effectively destroy reservations by removing federal protection. States could then move in to take Indian land through prohibitive taxes and other laws. Tribal governments as well as reservations communities and the economies that supported them were destroyed.

Books and Articles

Agnew, Brad. "Wilma Mankiller." In *The New Warriors: Native American Leaders since 1900*, edited by R. David Edmunds, 211–236. Lincoln, Nebr.: University of Nebraska Press, 2001.

Cadwalader, Sandra L., and Vine Deloria, Jr., eds. *The Aggressions of Civilization: Federal Indian Policy since the 1880s*. Philadelphia, Pa.: Temple University Press, 1984.

Calloway, Colin. *First Peoples: A Documentary Survey of American Indian History*. Boston, Mass.: Bedford/St. Martin's, 2004.

Cohen, Felix S. *Handbook of Federal Indian Law*. Washington, D.C.: Government Printing Office, 1942.

Collier, John. *The Indians of America*. New York: W. W. Norton and Company, 1947.

Deloria, Philip, and Neal Salisbury, eds. *A Companion to American Indian History*. Malden, Mass.: Blackwell Publishers, Inc., 2002.

Deloria, Vine, Jr., and Clifford M. Lytle. *American Indians, American Justice*. Austin, Tex.: University of Texas Press, 1983.

_____. *The Nations Within: The Past and Future of American Indian Sovereignty*. New York: Pantheon Books, 1984.

Edmunds, David R. "American History, Tecumseh, and the Shawnee Prophet." In *Major Problems in American Indian History*, edited by Albert L. Hurtado and Peter Iverson, 196–205. Lexington, Mass.: D.C. Heath and Company, 1994.

Finger, John. *The Eastern Band of Cherokees, 1819–1900*. Knoxville, Tenn.: University of Tennessee Press, 1984.

Fixico, Donald L. *The Urban Indian Experience in America*. Albuquerque, N.M.: University of New Mexico Press, 2000.

_____. *Urban Indians*. New York: Chelsea House Publishers, 1991.

Fowler, Loretta. *Tribal Sovereignty and the Historical Imagination: Cheyenne-Arapaho Politics*. Lincoln, Nebr.: University of Nebraska Press, 2002.

Gibson, Arrell Morgan. *The American Indian: Prehistory to the Present*. Lexington, Mass.: D.C. Heath and Company, 1980.

Grounds, Richard A., George E. Tinker, and David E. Wilkins. *Native Voices:*

American Indian Identity and Resistance. Lawrence, Kans.: University Press of Kansas, 2003.

Hagan, William T. *American Indians.* Chicago, Ill.: University of Chicago Press, 1961.

Harring, Sidney L. "Indian Law, Sovereignty, and State Law." In *A Companion to American Indian History,* edited by Philip J. Deloria and Neal Salisbury, 441–459. Malden, Mass.: Blackwell Publishers, Inc., 2002.

Hertzberg, Hazel W. *The Search for an American Indian Identity: Modern Pan-Indian Movements.* Syracuse, N.Y.: Syracuse University Press, 1971.

Hoxie, Frederick E. *A Final Promise: The Campaign to Assimilate the Indians, 1880–1920.* Lincoln, Nebr.: University of Nebraska Press, 2001.

Iverson, Peter. *Carlos Montezuma and the Changing World of American Indians,* 2nd Edition. Albuquerque, N.M.: University of New Mexico Press, 2001.

_____. *The Navajo Nation.* Albuquerque, N.M.: University of New Mexico Press, 1981.

_____. *The Navajos.* New York: Chelsea House Publishers, 1990.

_____, ed. *The Plains Indians of the Twentieth Century.* Norman, Okla.: University of Oklahoma Press, 1985.

Johnson, Kenneth. "Sovereignty, Citizenship and the Indian." *Arizona Law Review* 15 (1973): 973–1003.

Kelly, Lawrence C. *The Assault on Assimilation: John Collier and the Origins of Indian Policy Reform.* Albuquerque, N.M.: University of New Mexico Press, 1983.

_____. "The Indian Reorganization Act: The Dream and the Reality." In *The American Indian Past and Present,* edited by Roger Nichols, 242–255. New York: Alfred A. Knopf, 1986.

Kickingbird, Kirke, and Karen Ducheneaux. *One Hundred Million Acres.* New York: Macmillan Publishing Co, 1973. McNickle, D'Arcy. *Native American Tribalism: Indian Survivals and Renewals.* New York: Oxford University Press, 1973.

Metcalf, Warren. *Termination's Legacy: The Discarded Indians of Utah.* Lincoln, Nebr.: University of Nebraska Press, 2002.

Mintz, Steven, ed. *Native American Voices: A History and Anthology.* St. James, N.Y.: Brandywine Press, 1995.

Bibliography

Nabokov, Peter. *Native American Testimony*. New York: Penguin Putnam, Inc. 1999.

Nagel, Joane. *American Indian Ethnic Renewal: Red Power and the Resurgence of Identity and Culture*. New York: Oxford University Press, 1996.

Nichols, Roger, ed. *The American Indian Past and Present*. New York: Alfred A. Knopf, 1986.

Oklahoma's Poor Rich Indians. Philadelphia, Pa.: The Indian Rights Association, 1924.

Ourada, Patricia K. *The Menominee*. New York: Chelsea House Publishers, 1990.

Parker, Arthur C. *The Code of Handsome Lake*. Albany, N.Y.: New York State Museum, 1911, reprinted in 1990.

Philp, Kenneth. *John Collier's Crusade for Indian Reform, 1920–1934*. Tucson, Ariz.: University of Arizona Press, 1977.

Prucha, Francis Paul, ed. *Documents of United States Indian Policy*. Lincoln, Nebr.: University of Nebraska Press, 1975.

Stein, Gary. "The Indian Citizenship Act of 1924." *New Mexico Historical Review* 47 (Fall 1972): 257–274.

Thompson, William N. *Native American Issues: A Reference Handbook*. Santa Barbara, Calif.: ABC-CLIO, Inc. 1996.

Trafzer, Clifford E. *As Long as the Grass Shall Grow and Rivers Flow*. Fort Worth, Tex.: Harcourt College Publishers, 2000.

White, Benton R., and Christine Schultz White. "Phillip Martin: Mississippi Choctaw." In *The New Warriors: Native American Leaders since 1900*, edited by R. David Edmunds, 195–209. Lincoln, Nebr.: University of Nebraska Press, 2001.

Wise, Jennings C. *The Red Man in the New World Drama: A Politico-Legal Study with a Pageantry of American Indian History*. Washington, D.C.: W. F. Roberts Co., 1931.

Wunder, John R. "Walter Echo-Hawk." In *The New Warriors: Native American Leaders since 1900*, edited by R. David Edmunds, 299–321. Lincoln, Nebr.: University of Nebraska Press, 2001.

Books

Cornell, Stephen. *The Return of Native.* New York: Oxford University Press, 1989.

Deloria, Vine, Jr., and David E. Wilkins. *Tribes, Treaties, and Constitutional Tribulations.* Austin, Tex.: University of Texas Press, 2000.

Rosier, Paul C. *Rebirth of the Blackfeet Nation, 1912–1954*: Lincoln, Nebr.: University of Nebraska Press.

Wilkins, David. *American Indian Politics and the American Political System.* Lanham, Md.: Rowman and Littlefield.

_____, and Lomawaima, K. Tsianina. *Uneven Ground: American Indian Sovereignty and Federal Law.* Norman, Okla.: University of Oklahoma Press, 2001.

Wilkinson, Charles. *American Indians, Time, and the Law.* New Haven, Conn.: Yale University Press, 1987.

Websites

www.asu.edu/lib/archives/links.htm

This website sponsored by Arizona State University provides one of the most complete set of links this author has found on the Internet. Teachers interested in all American Indian issues should consult this resource.

www.cherokee.org

The official website of the Cherokee Nation offers a number of teaching tools for classroom use as well as the latest tribal news. A recent welcome addition has been the establishment of an online language course for those wishing to learn to speak Tsalagi.

www.cradleboard.org

The Cradleboard Teaching Project was founded by Buffy Sainte-Marie to provide social studies teachers with classroom-ready lesson plans. These are organized for elementary school (grades 3–5), middle school (grades 6–8), and high school (grades 9–12) instruction.

www.dpi.state.wi.us/amind/index.html

The State of Wisconsin now requires that its public school social studies curriculum include instruction on American Indian culture. Teachers in other states wishing to learn more about the curriculum established by the Department of Public Instruction in Wisconsin can find it here.

www.geotrees.com/nightwolf.html

Jay Winter Nightwolf, a Washington, D.C., area American Indian offers a weekly radio program that examines many current economic and social issues in Indian Country. His broadcast may be heard on Sunday evenings over the Internet at http://www.wpfw.org/. His past guests have included tribal officials, as well as leading advocates from groups like the National Congress of American Indians.

www.humboldt.edu/~go1/kellogg/NativeRelationship.html

This site provides access to American Indian Issues: An Introductory and Curricular Guide for Educators developed by the American Indian Civics project and funded by the W.K. Kellogg Foundation's Native American Higher Education Initiative. Here one may find succinct summaries of a variety of issues dealing with American Indian peoples' history and current development. The site includes both unit and lesson plans for classroom use.

www.indiancountry.com

This site provides an online version of the United States' largest American Indian newspaper, *Indian Country Today*, published weekly.

www.hanksville.org/Naresources/

This site provides an extensive virtual library on a host of American Indian issues.

http://www.h-net.msu.edu/

Perhaps the most valuable web resource for teachers interested in learning more about American Indian peoples today can be found through H-NET, a service of Michigan State University. To register, contact H-AMINDIAN@ H-NET.MSU.EDU. Operated by a very capable staff at Arizona State University, H-AMINDIAN will send the latest news releases from wire services, relevant publications, and comments by individuals, for the most part teachers in American Indian studies.

http://jaie.asu.edu/

The *Journal of American Indian Education* is available through subscription. Its on-line site offers a synopsis of all volumes back to 1961.

www.narf.org

> The website of the Native American Rights Fund, dedicated to providing legal representation and assistance to Indian tribes, communities, and individuals. Its goals include protecting tribal existence, natural resources, and Indian rights. To that end, they undertake court cases, promote litigation, and assist in negotiations to compel U.S. government accountability, as well as educating the public about Indian laws and issues.

www.nativeweb.com

> Current news about issues affecting indigenous peoples worldwide may be found on this site, which also provides a multitude of links for information on economic and other issues.

www.newberry.org/mcnickle/darcyhome.html

> The D'Arcy McNickle Center for American Indian History at the Newberry Library in Chicago remains one of the best archives in the nation.

www.osu-okmulgee.edu/faculty_and_staff/carsten_schmidtke/indian.htm

> An older site that is very user-friendly for teachers and students alike has been created by Carsten Schmidtke at Oklahoma State University–Okmulgee and offers a multitude of links.

www.sni.org

> To learn more about the continuing controversy between New York and its Seneca peoples, one may read the latest news at this website of the Seneca Nation.

www.usgs.gov/features/native_americans.html

> The United States Geographical Service offers a valuable series of photographs from the Blue Cloud Abbey Native American Photograph collection. Most of these photographs depict early-twentieth-century life in and around the Yankton Sioux Reservation in southeastern South Dakota.

Films on American Indian Sovereignty

Imagining Indians. Victor Masayesva, Jr. (1992, 60 minutes).
    Deals with issues of sovereignty and representation.
In Light of Reverence. Christopher McLeod. (2001, 74 minutes).
    Focuses on tribal land rights.

In Whose Honor? Jay Rosenstein (1997, 47 minutes).

> Primarily examines the use of mascots, exploring issues of Indian sovereignty in trying to exert control over imagery.

The Menominee. Schlessinger Media (1998, 30 minutes)

> A history of the Menominee Indians of Wisconsin that includes their reclamation of land following Termination. This video was prepared as part of the INDIANS OF NORTH AMERICA series. Other titles (all 30 minutes in length) include: *The Chinook, The Creek, The Crow, The Huron, The Narragansett,* and *The Pueblo.*

Usual and Accustomed Places. Sandra Sunrising Osawa (2002, 48 minutes).

> Examines issues of sovereignty and fishing rights.

Index

Indian Tribal Government Tax Status
    Act, 96
Indian Trust Fund, 79
Inter-marriage, 18, 51
Iroquois, 4, 7, 19, 49
Iwo Jima, 29, 30

Jackson, Andrew, 21–22, 83, 89, 100
Jandreau, Michael, 98
Jefferson, Thomas, 16
Jena Band of Choctaws, 97
Jim Crow Laws, 90
Johnson, Caleb, 107
Johnson, Lyndon B., 32
Johnson, William (Sir), 11

Kennedy, John F., 32
Knox, Henry, 15, 16, 18

Language, 6
Lewis, Meriwether, 16–17, 18
Lewis, Virgil, 77
Livingston, Robert, 16
Louisiana Territory, 16, 17
Lumbee tribe, 53

MacDonald, Peter, 66, 69
    his achievements, 67
    his prison sentence, 68
Maine, 98
Maine Indian Claims Settlement Act,
    82
Major Crimes Act, 73–74, 105, 108
Marshall, John (Chief Justice), 23, 85,
    104–105
Martin, Phillip (Chief), 63, 64, 88
Masayesva, Vernon, 106–107
McCloud, Janet, 109–110
McIntosh, William, 71
Menominees, 57–58, 90, 100
Métis, 9
Mexico, 4
Mississippi Band of Choctaw, 102–103
Mississippi Valley, 6
Missouri River, 17

Mohawk, 7, 11
Mohawk Council of Akwesasne, 71
Mohawk Nation Council of Chiefs, 71
Monk's Mound, 5
Montana v. United States, 76
Montezuma, Carlos, 36, 37, 38, 39–40,
    78, 80
Murphy, Mike, 101
Museum of the American Indian, 105

Nabokov, Peter, 51
Nakai, Raymond, 67
Napoleon, 16
Nation (Tribe), 2
National American Indian Court
    Judges Association
    and categories into which tribal gov-
    ernments fall, 57
National American Indian Housing
    Council, 62
National Congress of American
    Indians (NCAI), 43, 47
National Council of American Indians
    (NCAI), 40, 41, 42, 83
National Indian Defense Association,
    35
National Indian Gaming Commission
    (NIGC), 95, 101
National Indian Youth Council, 44
National Museum of the American
    Indian, 62–63
Native American Church, 42
Native American Rights Fund (NARF),
    81–82, 90, 102, 107–108
Navajo Agricultural Products Industry,
    67
Navajo Forest Products Industry, 67
Navajos, 3, 24, 49, 50, 56, 66–70, 107
Navajo Times, 69
New Mexico, 84, 90
New York State Department of
    Taxation, 93
Nixon, Richard, 68
    his message on Indian Affairs, 32
Northern Cheyenne tribe, 102

Deborah Welch, Ph.D., is Director of the Public History Program and Associate Professor of History at Longwood University. Welch has published numerous books and articles, including *Virginia: An Illustrated History* (Hippocrene Books); "Zitkala-Sa," which appeared in *American National Biography* (Oxford University Press), and "Gertrude Simmons Bonnin," which appeared in *The New Warriors: American Leaders since 1900*. Her fictional academic murder mysteries are set among American Indian peoples and appear under the pseudonym P.D. Lawrence.

Paul C. Rosier received his Ph.D. in American History from the University of Rochester, with a specialty in Native American History. His first book, *Rebirth of the Blackfeet Nation, 1912–1954*, was published by the University of Nebraska Press in 2001. In November 2003, Greenwood Press published *Native American Issues* as part of its Contemporary American Ethnic Issues series. Dr. Rosier has also published articles on Native American topics in the *American Indian Culture and Research Journal*, and the *Journal of American Ethnic History*. In addition, he was coeditor of *The American Years: A Chronology of United States History*. He is Professor of History at Villanova University, where he also serves as a faculty advisor to the Villanova Native American Student Association.

Walter Echo-Hawk is a member of the Pawnee tribe. He is a staff attorney of the Native American Rights Fund (*www.narf.org*) and a Justice on the Supreme Court of the Pawnee Nation (*www.pawnee nation.org/court*). He has handled cases and legislation affecting Native American rights in areas such as religious freedom, education, water rights, fishing rights, grave protection, and tribal repatriation of Native dead.